FISHING NOWADAYS

Also by George Brennand

HALCYON

AN ANGLER'S MEMORIES

FISHING NOWADAYS

BY

GEORGE BRENNAND

WITH EIGHTEEN PHOTOGRAPHS

ADAM & CHARLES BLACK
4, 5 & 6 SOHO SQUARE LONDON W.1

FIRST PUBLISHED 1951

MADE IN GREAT BRITAIN
PRINTED BY WESTERN PRINTING SERVICES, LTD., BRISTOL

CONTENTS

Part I
ON THE CATCHING OF TROUT

Part II
ON THE CATCHING OF SALMON

Part III
ON THE CATCHING OF SEA TROUT

ILLUSTRATIONS

PART I

ON THE CATCHING OF TROUT

CHAPTER I

ON FISHING AS A SPORT

THERE can be very little doubt that fishing for sport—
what might be termed the Waltonian Cult—produces,
and has for long produced, a richer crop of eccentrics,
pleasant companions and happy men than all the
other "field sports" put together. This is particularly
so, I think, in Great Britain, which is still the home and
"inner circle", as it were, of the world-wide Waltonian
religion. Curiously enough, the actual catching of
fish, or at any rate the habitual and successful catching
of fish, has very little to do with the quiet delights of
"going fishing". All over the world, ragged boys with
home-made rods and multi-millionaires with the latest
products of Hardy or Leonard may be observed
gazing happily into silent, nameless pools or casting
persistently over the singing streams of great and
famous rivers. They have Faith, these happy people,
and a certainty in their hearts that, if they can catch
nothing else, they will at least capture contentment
and peace of mind.

The great army of what might be called "guild-
fishers", the members of the working-men's fishing

clubs, who line so many rivers and canals during the
week-end, seem to care very little about what they
catch, but are content to be just fishing. . . .

On tropical summer middays and on blizzard-
swept December afternoons, thousands of these hardy
fishers contrive to amuse themselves at very little cost,
and without injury to any man.

Fishing for sport is probably the most truly demo-
cratic occupation known to man. Many a duke has
been known to gaff a fish for his own ghillie and many a
ghillie has been heard to curse a duke for not playing
a fish in the right way. Izaak Walton, the plain, old,
retired haberdasher, was always "the Master" to
Charles Cotton, the young and rather raffish Cavalier-
Squire.

The true fishers are very little affected by social
changes, and the capitalist may ruin a river through
polluting it or a poacher improve a stream by reducing
the fish population, and then restocking it with a
neighbouring landowner's newly-bought Loch Levens.
And yet this contention is not quite as true as it seems,
for in fact, social changes do bring and have brought
about great alterations in the past century.

There is, for example, much more fishing available
to the general public than, say, fifty years ago, while
at the same time the fishing itself is on the whole not as
good as formerly. There has been and will be much
controversial argument about this, but I personally
am convinced that those who contend that our rivers
and streams are swiftly becoming unfishable through
pollution, over-fishing and other causes are just as
wrong in their contentions as are those who hold that
"public ownership" would mean more and better
fishing for all.

The fact is that fishing, like everything else, is constantly changing. Some fishing in some places is much better than of old, while in some places the fishing is very much worse.

Rivers that once were famous are now fetid drains devoid of all fish life, while streams that were once mere reed- and weed-choked rivulets are now very perfect trout streams. And so it goes on, the arguments "about it and about", while the "honest men and fishermen" still enjoy their ancient sport.

There is one happy fact, however, which has become noticeable in recent years; the brief reign of the purist seems to be passing. Among fly-fishermen the great gulf which once, for a few years, yawned between the "dry-fly men" and the "chuck and chance it" pundits has closed, we hope, for ever. No longer, even in the sun-smitten fishing huts of Wessex, is the user of a nymph looked upon as a dabbler in black magic. No longer do lifelong friends cut each other in the street because of an argument about the use of a wet fly. . . .

The only fighting point which remains is the comparatively modern controversy about the thread-line reel and its various uses. Even this argument only flares up occasionally when some new method is suggested. . . .

The only real purists left are, curiously enough, the "working-men" fishermen of England who, unlike their opposite numbers in Scotland or Wales, are still inclined to stick obstinately to their fishing stools, baskets of tackle and bait, and their age-old, sedentary practice of "studying to be quiet". But then the English working man is essentially conservative!

I once belonged to a working-men's club that rented a delightful length of river which the members stocked most carefully and at great expense. Despite the fact

that most of their water consisted largely of lovely open
flats, admirably suited to the use of a dry-fly, my
fellow members insisted upon sitting behind bushes
with their rods supported on forked sticks, while they
"ledgered" with maggots and worms in the deep
pools. This arrangement suited me very well, as I had
the greater part of the fishing to myself. The fact that
I habitually caught more and larger trout than most
of the other members did not appear to interest them
at all. . . .

I asked one of my fellow members why he persisted
in sitting all afternoon watching a motionless float
while I was catching three or four brace of nice trout
on a May fly. He replied that fly-fishing always seemed
to him "too much like work". . . . Maybe he was
right, but I still think that their "purism" is standing
between them and much good sport.

There is one sort of fishing that has changed very
much in the past few decades, and that is salmon
fishing. The breaking up of so many big estates and
the acquisition by hotels and fishing clubs of much
water, formerly most jealously preserved and guarded
by private proprietors, has made the catching of salmon
by the casual fisherman of moderate means a much
more practicable and much less expensive business
than of old.

Even twenty years ago it was very difficult to enjoy
good salmon fishing except on expensive rivers, while
nowadays there are hotel fishings which are really
good. There are a number of fishing associations that
provide absolutely first-class fishing on weekly or
monthly or annual tickets at a fraction of the cost that
one would have paid for a "lease" in the old days. The
fishing may not be quite as good as formerly, and the
pools may suffer from over-fishing, but for the man

who can spend only a modest amount, this modern development is a great improvement.

When one comes to the point of writing a book about how and where to fish, one is immediately confronted by the problem of how to deal with controversial matters without being offensive, and to suggest original (if possible) ways of fishing without being accused of being a "poacher". As to where to fish, one can, I think, merely make suggestions about places where one has actually fished oneself, or where one's friends have fished recently.

It is almost impossible to achieve complete accuracy in this matter, as rivers change within the space of one season from excellence to mediocrity. Fishings which have for many years been strictly private suddenly become "ticket" waters, or club waters private fishings once more. The question of where to stay is another rather difficult matter to treat with accuracy. An admirable hotel may change hands and become very far from admirable within a very brief period, while the most indifferent "pub" becomes an ideal fishing inn.

My aim in this book has been to help those who wish to become true fishermen, and to enjoy the most delightful of all sports. I have written more for the man of modest means than for the rich man, and more for the lover of quiet country and peace than for the man who strives to make "records". I have tried to stress the truth that the real enjoyment of fishing lies more in the actual fishing itself than in the catching of fish, although this may seem at first almost a paradox.

In the section dealing with where to fish, I have purposely chosen places which I know possess much charm and beauty, even if the fishing in some instances is not first-class. It is better to find some hotel or inn where the "atmosphere" is congenial to the fisherman, and where he can catch small trout or an occasional salmon or sea trout in beautiful surroundings, than to become for a period the slave of some highly efficient but unpeaceful fishing manager who will "see to it" that you achieve what he considers to be your just quota of slaughter.

Freedom is, I think, the thing that most British fishermen appreciate most in their sport, and even in the peaceful pursuit of angling this has sometimes to be fought for. The urge to "plan", to limit and to manage is, I fear, a growing tendency in modern life that the true fisherman must always be ready to counteract. Therefore, avoid the fanatic like the plague, and go to your fishing with an open mind, for there you will find happiness.

CHAPTER II

TO THOSE THINKING OF "TAKING UP" FISHING

FOR years I have been meeting people who tell me they are thinking of "taking up" fishing, or "learning" to fish, or that they would so much like to fish.

To those over-humble souls, of whom there are many, who really do want to fish, but who seem to suffer from a kind of inferiority complex about it, I would like to say a few well-meaning but possibly presumptuous words.

In the first place, do not look upon fishing as some sort of "subject" that has to be studied as if for the ultimate passing of an examination. You will not learn much about fishing from books until you are actually a fisherman yourself. It is fishermen who love reading fishing books.

Personally, I think there is far too much insistence, in some fishing books, upon casting and the various mechanical processes connected with fishing, and too little mention of the principles of the sport. After all, there are any amount of expert casters of a fly or a bait who are in no sense true fishermen.

Very many great and notable fishers have been and are comparatively ordinary or at any rate quite unspectacular casters both of a fly and a minnow. Obviously, it is no use making wonderful and perfect casts in a place where there are no salmon lying, or to place a beautifully cast dry-fly over a trout that is not "on the fin". Quite a number of would-be fishers, especially those who take the sport up in middle age, spend a vast amount of money and trouble in fitting themselves up with the most perfect rods and tackle, before they have even learned to put a fly on the water properly, or mastered the all-important art of "seeing fish".

Now this matter of being able to look into the water, as it were, as apart from looking on to the water, is, in my opinion, probably the most important single requisite for being a fisherman. Very many people, even people who do occasionally fish, can walk along a river all day without seeing a single fish. I have even known those who could do this while a good, steady rise was in progress, and still be quite unconscious that there was even one trout rising.

A year or two ago I was fishing one day on a small river in the North Midlands. I had hooked and landed perhaps a dozen trout, four or five of which were worth keeping. I had also watched for two hours a remarkable rise of trout in the rough water of the streams. Encountering an acquaintance of mine who had "taken up" fishing that season, he astounded me by greeting me with the remark that he hadn't seen a trout rise all day.

This seeing of trout and the rises of trout is much more a matter of knowing what to look for than of good eye sight. I once knew a well-known fisher of grayling and trout in a Yorkshire river who was actually very short-sighted, and wore thick-lens glasses, and yet I have seen him hooking fish after fish when the light was beginning to fade—with a tiny dry-fly—on really rough and rapid streams.

I always advise any of my friends who are thinking of taking an interest in fishing just to start by walking along some good length of river, watching the fish, and the birds, without attempting to fish at all. . . . After doing this for a time their senses, generally, will gradually "take up the tune", as it were, of the river, and their eyes will begin to see things, and understand them, that they never knew existed. They will be able to distinguish between the plop of a vole just under the bank from the sound of a trout rising in the same sort of place, or the rise of a good trout from the very similar disturbance of a pool made by a dipper. They will be able to stand and stare down into the deep tail of a run and after a few minutes their eyes will focus themselves until they can see perhaps half a dozen trout, where at first glance there appeared to be nothing at all. On the whole, salmon are much harder to see than brown trout, and sea trout are, generally speaking, the hardest to see of any fish.

When the beginner has reached the point where he can see fish and observe readily a rise of trout in a rippling river, it will be time enough for him to start fishing. I should advise him to buy a good, but not necessarily expensive, greenheart rod—not too whippy and of a weight which seems to him light in the hand; a rod, moreover, that is well balanced by the reel and line. A reel balances a rod when the whole rod, with the line pulled through the ring, and with a yard or two hanging down from the tip, balances exactly on a finger, at the point where the cork handle meets the rod itself. I would also suggest that the beginner see to it that he has a really good, well-dressed line, and, if anything, let it be on the heavy side for the rod. A line that is too light makes casting infinitely more difficult for the novice. If there is any wind, a light line will make him feel that the whole process is utterly hopeless.

When he finds that he can flick a length of line, about twice the length of his rod, backwards and forwards in the air quite easily, let him then try to cast at some mark on the grass, at the same time keeping the elbow of his casting arm tightly pressed to his side. After a little practice he will find that he can quite easily control a decent length of line—just by using his wrist. When this happens, the novice can then take it that he can cast, and should sally forth for the catching of trout.

He probably won't catch any for the first day, but before long he will find that he is beginning to get a fly over, or somewhere near, some particular trout which he can see is "on the fin", and probably ready to rise, if not actually rising.

All the rest of the delightful and enthralling paraphernalia of the fisher will become his in the natural course of events, as he becomes more and more of a true fisher. Split-cane rods, nice reels, well-dressed lines, waders, fishing bags, nets, etc., endless boxes of flies and baits, all these the novice will find in his possession almost without knowing he has bought them. And then, maybe, he will buy a thread-line reel, and all that follows thereafter, and he will find another vista of very pleasant things stretching out before him.

And while all these nice possessions are accumulating in his smoke-room, he will find that he is beginning actually to catch things—trout that do really weigh three-quarters of a pound, or a pound, and not just "about a pound". . . . As for the gleaming salmon—that is purely a matter of opportunity—and a cheque book. The fishing part of the performance will probably be taken out of his hands almost entirely by his boatman or ghillie, but if by some lucky chance he who was once a novice does manage to hook a salmon all by himself, he will experience something quite unique in the way of thrills—he may even land it. . . . In any case, by this time he will be a fisherman, and nothing that can happen will ever prevent him from fishing wherever there is water and fish to be caught.

CHAPTER III

FLY-FISHING IN CLEAR STREAMS WITH DRY-FLY AND NYMPH

To become a specialist in fishing is, to my mind, to lessen, quite perceptibly, one's enjoyment; to become a purist in the extreme sense is a very foolish thing indeed.

Despite this, I am well aware that very many true fishermen do indeed come in the end to the conclusion that of all fishing real dry-fly fishing (which definitely includes the just use of a nymph or upstream wet-fly) is the most delightful.

This is not to say that the catching of large trout in clear water is the hardest or the most skilful form of angling. In my opinion dry-fly fishing is one of the easiest methods of catching trout for the experienced and competent fisherman.

It may be that this statement will be contested by many better fishermen than I am, but nevertheless I think that if they will give the matter a little careful and honest thought, they will come to the conclusion that I am not so very far wrong. It is this general and, as I think, rather facile belief that dry-fly fishing is difficult that prevents very many beginners from even attempting it.

I think a good deal of this mistaken belief has arisen through the meticulous and sometimes rather precious literature on the subject which has come to be looked upon as somehow "classic". Quite unintentionally, many writers on chalk-stream fishing have conveyed the impression that the trout of the famous Test or Kennet fishings are endowed, to a much greater extent than all other trout, with almost human intelligence and a truly diabolic cunning.

The great and uncatchable trout of the club fishing has become almost a tradition in innumerable books and articles on angling. It naturally arises from this that the great trout must be approached with almost religious caution and tempted by beautifully tied flies which must be cast with mathematical precision and subtlety.

It is at about this point in the story that the inevitable gibe at "shop-tied flies" is introduced. . . . Ultimately the great trout suffers one of two fates. Either he is caught by some almost unbelievably accomplished fisher, or, as a notable contrast, by some clumsy novice who by some unexplained method manages to overcome the great trout's years of "education".

All this is complete nonsense. I would urge anyone who feels so inclined and is lucky enough to have the opportunity, to put the matter to the test and see what happens—even if he has only been fishing for a few months. The result may well surprise him.

There are, of course, times and seasons when *all* trout are more or less uncatchable by any means except a net. To begin with—many chalk-stream trout go completely off, as far as taking surface feed is concerned, for some weeks after the great fly hatches of June. Apart from the Mayfly hatches, June is a notable month for hatches of every kind of fly, and the trout in many rivers seem to make July a month of fasting except perhaps for a few nice juicy sedges every evening just about twilight.

When one thinks of their gluttonous behaviour during the Mayfly weeks, this is surely not to be wondered at. Anybody, whether a virtuoso of forty years' standing or one who has only just bought his first rod, can repair to the pleasant town of Hungerford in July or August and prove this for himself. . . . He will observe quite a number of very large trout in the Kennet and in the Dun, apparently made of wood. But to return to the actual catching of these fabulous denizens of our chalk streams. . . .

The first thing to do, I would suggest in all humility, is to walk quietly—*very quietly*—up the length of stream which you are about to fish. It is very necessary in this exercise to keep back, as far as possible, from the bank, and not to carry your rod so that it towers eight or nine feet above your head. A trout can see a rod as well, perhaps better, than you can.

If the sun is shining, which is quite possible even during an English summer, extreme care should be taken that neither your own nor your rod's shadow should fall on the water. The main thing to remember when walking up a stream is that *vibration* is by far the greatest danger-signal in the fish-world. As long as you keep *below* the angle of vision of a trout, no amount of vibrationless movement will frighten him, but the slightest vibration will cause him to go down, temporarily, "off the fin". Personally, I always walk softly and carefully up the length of water I mean to fish and mark down the trout that I hope to try for. In doing this it is best to take various actual marks on the bank such as a clump of thistles or reeds exactly opposite the head of the trout which you hope to cast over; when the time comes for actually making the cast it is not always possible to be in a position to see your fish.

In this sort of fishing I am quite convinced that the very finest gut cast is almost a necessity. I myself always use three-yard casts tapered to 5X; 4X, I think, is quite heavy enough to hold any fish if you carry out the right drill when playing him, and if you have reasonable luck. You will be broken just as effectively if you are using 3X or even 2X if your trout gets round a snag or a rock, or has a chance of using sufficiently strong weed stems. In any case, if a trout "weeds" you thoroughly, you are just as likely to be able to deal with him when using 5X gut as with any cast weaker than sea trout strength.

In casting over the two-pounder which you have so carefully marked down, try to do it in such a way that the junction knot of your reel-line and cast hits the water first, and the fly is therefore likely to "blow" down on to the water very gently. With a little practice this can be done so that a fly drops almost as quietly as a piece of thistledown.

Cast obliquely upstream in such a way that the fly only floats over or near the fish's head, never let the *gut* float over a fish first if you can avoid it.

The best position to cast from is a crouching or kneeling position when you are situated almost, but not quite, level with your trout; say on a line about three or four yards below his tail. If you are kneeling or crouching in this position, you will be *below* the trout's "window" of vision, and, if at the same time, you have managed to avoid any vibration, it is any old odds that the trout will remain totally unaware of your presence.

I have purposely stressed this question of approach and method of casting, because I am convinced that these factors are infinitely more important than the type of fly you eventually show to the trout.

I am well aware that many far more experienced
fishers than I have stressed the vital importance of
having the right fly; the fly, in fact, which is "on the
water", but I can only state what is my own personal
experience in the matter.

I never quite know what is meant by the "fly on the
water", because on most or maybe on all occasions
there are many different sorts of fly actually on the
water and my own experience is that trout, more
often than not, take all sorts of different flies within
the space of, say, twenty minutes—if they are really
feeding.

This is notably the case when the Mayflies are
coming down. I have seen the whole river covered
with Mayflies, and trout rising greedily—but not at
the Mayflies, although a casual observer would very
likely think that the rise *was* at Mayflies. Trout very
often splash at and play with the Mayflies floating
down, while they are really feeding steadily on duns
which are also on the water. As to the fly to use at
any given time, it is naturally a good thing to use a
darkish dun such as a Greenwell if you have actually
observed that the trout are *really* feeding on darkish
Olives of a similar type.

However, in my experience a trout really "on the
fin" and rising steadily will more often than not take a
nicely presented Tup or Variant, even if he has, in fact,
been feeding steadily on Iron Blues or Olives.

It seems to me that in this respect a trout is probably
no different from a man. If one has been expecting
to be brought some rather "tired" chicken, I do not
think one would object if the waiter announced that
there was no more chicken, but that, in its place, the
chef had conjured up a nice roast grouse! In the same
way, I cannot think why a trout that has been feeding

LOCH MOIDART WITH CASTLE TIRRIM, INVERNESS-SHIRE

JUNCTION OF TEST AND ANTON AT FULLERTON ("SEVEN STARS")

see a whole wide "ford" of Tweed simply boiling with feeding trout; times when the March Browns and snow-flakes seem all mixed up together, and wading up to one's waist in long waders is an exercise for Spartans.

But it is from the end of April onwards when the upstream fisher of a dry-fly or a nymph comes into his own. In the "old days" the local Tweed or Coquet trout fisherman practically ceased to fish after April, except perhaps with a worm during "dirty" floods.

Nowadays, if one knows one's river reasonably well, it is possible to enjoy really good sport, wading up-stream and dropping a floating fly or a nymph in all likely places, or over actual rises.

Now in this kind of dry-fly fishing it is rarely possible to see fish well, or at all, and it needs con-siderable judgment to gauge exactly where a trout is lying, even when one has seen him rise. It also re-quires a good deal of practical fishing experience to know where trout are likely to be lying. It is for these reasons that I contend that it takes a much better and more experienced fisher to catch good trout either with a dry-fly or wet on the so-called "rough streams" than on an orthodox chalk stream.

I would, therefore, recommend a beginner to start, if he is lucky enough to be able to do so, where he will probably end his career as an elderly "expert", that is to say, on one of the well-known chalk or limestone streams. . . . He will, if he does this, get used to seeing, watching and studying trout; he will also learn how and when a trout actually takes a fly or nymph. Until he has considerable experience of this sort, he will find that his dry-fly fishing on the rough, fast streams is not too successful.

As far as nymph fishing is concerned, very nearly all the foregoing remarks apply—except that the so-called

"fly" you are using will be fished under the water
instead of on the surface.

I am quite certain that almost any lightly dressed
dry-fly or, for that matter, many ordinary wet-flies,
will serve your purpose, as long as it is presented in the
right way.

Having marked down and approached your trout,
and observed that although he is "on the fin", he is
feeding below the surface, you will notice that if this
is happening, your selected fish will be seen to be
darting to the left or right or upstream while feeding,
instead of just rising to the surface to take floating
flies.

It is a good thing when casting over a feeding fish
with a nymph to use glycerine on the fly, and about
two feet of the cast, so that it will sink well before it
actually reaches the trout. In nymph fishing exactly
the same thing applies as in fishing dry—get almost
level with the trout, kneel down below his "window"
of vision and cast in such a way that the fly alone is
seen by the trout. The only difference is that you must
drop the fly rather more upstream of your fish than
when using a floating fly, as the process of sinking takes
an appreciable time to happen even when glycerine
is used.

There is a third method which I have found to be
very deadly on certain occasions in this type of fishing.
In effect, it is neither true dry-fly fishing nor true
nymph fishing, but a combination of both. Instead of
floating your fly over the trout or swimming your
nymph down to him, use an ordinary dry-fly without
any grease or scentless paraffin on it, and *damp* it
slightly before you actually cast. When you do cast,
try to drop the fly quite a long way upstream of the
trout.

The fly will begin to become water-logged almost as soon as it touches the water. When it has floated down to a point about two yards upstream of the trout, give it a few very slight and quick jerks. This will cause the water-logged fly to dart below the surface at just about the moment when it is observed by the trout. Very frequently he will dart straight at it and take firmly.

I have found this method, which, by the way, is not by any means quite as easy as the ordinary dry-fly technique, to be very useful at times when the trout are particularly fastidious and "purist" about taking in the ordinary way.

CHAPTER IV

FLY-FISHING ON SCOTTISH, NORTHERN AND WESTERN RIVERS

ATHOUGH I personally think that a floating fly fished upstream is more often than not a more satisfactory method than the older downstream wet-fly technique, I am well aware that vast numbers of people, particularly in Scotland, still enjoy wet-fly fishing more than any other sort of angling.

This downstream fishing with two or more flies on a cast is, of course, a type of nymph fishing, and is, therefore, quite successful on days when very few trout are actually showing on the surface. Conversely, it is frequently rather disappointing on days when there is an obvious hatch of surface duns, and the trout are splashing about all over the river.

The vast majority of anglers still use the wet-fly technique when loch fishing; it is, on most occasions, more successful than dry-fly fishing. However, I will come to the question of loch fishing later on.

I think one of the reasons that very many people prefer the fishing of a wet-fly on rough streams is the element of surprise and uncertainty. There is, in fact, a distinct flavour of gambling about this casting more or less blindly into water which may produce nothing, a diminutive salmon parr, or a beautiful trout of two pounds or more.

The old-time dry-fly purist's jeer about the "chuck

and chance it method" is about three-quarters utter nonsense, and about a quarter true. There is, of course, a certain element of "chuck and chance" about it. Very little skill in casting is required, and chance does indeed play a good part in the result. Nevertheless, a really good and experienced fisherman on the Tweed or Coquet, or on the rivers of Lancashire and Yorkshire, has, more often than not, a very shrewd idea as to where the trout are lying, and whether he is fishing over a likely taking place or not. Frequently he also knows of the existence, in certain places, of good trout that he has seen rise, sometimes in very awkward places, too.

To the novice at this sort of fishing, I would like to stress one or two points.

Always fish more across the current than down it. I would even go so far as to suggest that it is better to cast slightly upstream and across. The longer the flies are washing down the stream without any drag, the longer time there will be during which a taking rise is probable. The fish that take you when the flies are dragging more or less downstream and below you are usually very small trout or salmon parr.

One of the most likely places for a good trout is in the deep, fast water where the main current flows right along one bank. If there are also some over-hanging trees or bushes, so much the better. This applies more after April than before it. In March and early April on most northern rivers, the good trout are frequently to be found in the fast shallow water of the "fords". This is particularly the case when the stone-flies are hatching out.

When wet-fly fishing on the big border rivers or in Scotland generally, one can use a good deal heavier cast than in chalk-stream fishing, despite the fact that the average trout caught is very unlikely to exceed half a pound. If you use, say, 5X gut, it is surprising how often you can be broken even by small trout. It must be remembered that a lively three-quarter-pound trout in heavy spring water can frequently exercise a breaking strain very much greater than that produced by even a two-pound or three-pound trout in a quiet southern stream.

In any case, when you have to bring a trout upstream to the net, and you are hoping, perhaps, to get four or five brace of trout in the day, it is no good wasting too much time. If, of course, you happen to hook a really big trout, it is better to wade out to a suitable shingle beach and play him from there.

Incidentally, if you happen to be fishing from this same shingle beach, it is quite unnecessary to use your net at all. If you keep a strong pressure on the fish and walk backwards across the river, you will find that the trout, even a two-pound fish, will kick himself up on to dry land in the most obliging manner.

There is, in fact, very little special technical knowledge about wet-fly fishing which can be adequately dealt with in print. The best way to become a good wet-fly fisherman is just to fish. There are dozens of little subtleties and tricks which are almost unexplainable, and which will become part of a keen fisher's repertoire quite automatically.

There is also very little to be said, I think, about wet-fly fishing on lochs. It is almost essential in this sort of fishing to have someone rowing you who is used to "keeping" a boat. I would go so far as to say that this is the one really vital factor in loch fishing. Incidentally, it is usually very little good fishing a loch from the shore, as loch trout almost always feed just where the shallow shelves away into the deep, and this is more often than not well out of reach from the shore.

There are exceptions to this rule, of course. Some lochs can be fished by wading, and some few from the shore itself, but on the whole it can be taken as an axiom that a boat and a good boatman are essential.

Local knowledge is almost more useful on a loch than on most rivers, and an experienced local ghillie or boatman will know just where the best "drifts" are situated.

In many lochs there are submerged ridges and rocks right out in the middle where one would naturally expect only deep water. Drifts along these ridges and over these rocky shallows are often very good indeed. On the whole, I think the main points to be remembered about fishing a loch are that the very deep water is quite useless, and that usually the fish rise near the shore on to which the wind is blowing.

Although I have, I suppose, caught very large numbers of trout in lochs and lakes with a wet-fly, I must own that I think the time-honoured technique of drifting in a more or less perishing wind, casting eternally into a waste of waters, is the least idyllic and least artistic of all forms of fishing. It seems to me to need less skill and to be more a pure gamble than even spring-bait fishing for salmon—which is saying a great deal.

Fishing lochs in various other and, I think, much more pleasant ways is quite another matter, about which I will hold forth later on.

CHAPTER V

THREAD-LINE FISHING FOR TROUT AND CHUB, AND THE USE OF A LIVE MINNOW

THE angling technique which in later years has come to be known as thread-line fishing has been known and practised in various forms for centuries. All sorts of methods have been used, from the coiling of a fine oiled line on to a tray carried round the fisherman's neck, like the Pieman's tray of our nursery rhyme days; a line coiled on to the flat stern of a punt or boat —to the reversible "Malloch" type of casting-reel of more recent years.

However, the invention of the "Illingworth" reel, and the eloquent advocacy of Mr. Alexander Wanless within the last fifteen or twenty years, have opened up what amounts to a completely new field in the angling world.

The uses of a fixed-spool reel are so many and varied that it would be boring to mention them all. Personally, although I am happiest when using a dry-fly and a 5X cast over large and cunning trout, I have found the very greatest amusement in experimenting with this type of fishing. Every fishing novice should make himself a present of a good thread-line reel at the earliest possible moment, and with it one or two books by Mr. Wanless on the subject. The outlay (quite considerable these days) will amply repay him.

Apart from the use with a fixed-spool reel of a spun minnow, either natural or artificial, I have found that the very greatest fun can be had casting a worm or live minnow on hot, still days when other forms of fishing are hopeless, upstream over trout which one has already marked down as on the move.

Although at the moment I am supposed to be writing about trout, I must, in connection with this form of fishing, include the noble and logger-headed chub, as in suitable water I think large chub are as difficult to catch and a good deal harder to land than the ordinary run of trout.

The methods and tackle required for the catching of trout with a thread-line have been so fully and competently dealt with by others in recent years that I do not feel myself experienced enough to lay down any laws on the subject. However, I would like to describe the methods I use for fishing a live minnow, which I have found to be very amusing.

From the end of June until September, the catching of trout with a fly becomes, in most places, a very uncertain, sometimes a disappointing, business.

The first half of July, however, is the ideal time for practising a type of fishing which has always given me a great amount of amusement—and some very good trout indeed. I refer to the artistic use of a live minnow —particularly in lakes or the lynns of Wales. This method of fishing is also very pleasant on many coarse-fishing rivers in places where the chub are large, and there are also a few good trout, which is often the case.

In many places, at this period of the year, it will be observed that great shoals of minnow congregate in the shallows, especially on really hot, sunny days, and that the largest trout, frequently the largest trout one has seen all the season, are waiting out in the deeper water, feeding on any minnows that happen to move out from the shallows. Often, too, one sees big trout rushing across the shallows themselves, chasing the minnow shoals.

My outfit for this live-minnow fishing is extremely simple. An ordinary dry-fly rod, nine foot or ten foot—it doesn't matter at all—a thread-line reel, with two-pound B.S. "Monofilament" nylon, and a small treble hook, one yard above the hook, two or three split shot placed close together, or one light lead about as big as a small pea; a light quill float can also be used with advantage, but I personally do not do so.

Referring now to the fishing of, say, a lynn in Wales, on a hot, still day in early July, I would take up my position on a rocky promontory which juts out into the deep water, with at its base a nice, preferably weedy shallow on which the minnow shoals are clustering. On to one or two of the barbs of the treble hook I would place tiny sections of a small worm. The thing to do now is to drop the baited triangle among the clustering minnows, and when, as will immediately happen, dozens of minnows fight round the bait, jerk the triangle until a minnow is foul-hooked. When you lift the minnow out, do not touch it, but, slipping the line out of the pick-up, make a cast well out into the deep water.

As the minnow lands leave everything completely slack for about one minute, and watch the floating line. Very frequently you will see the line shoot and you will be into a good trout. If you are not taken while the line is slack, begin to wind in very slowly, drawing the minnow gently towards the rocky point on which you are standing. Very often you will be taken just as the minnow gets within a yard or so of the rock.

A year or two ago I was living in North Wales and frequently fished a beautiful lynn above the Lledr Valley where the trout were extraordinarily dour; in fact, very few were caught by anyone, although during the "beetle" season those who knew how did get a number of good trout with the natural insect. On the whole, however, most visitors had given this lynn up as hopeless.

This lake was ideal for the type of minnow fishing I have been describing, with any amount of rocky promontories and shallows absolutely black with swarming minnows.

One hot day I walked up to see if I could get one of the big trout I had noticed occasionally splashing at the large sedges that now and then "feathered" out from the heathery banks—a variation of diet, I imagine, from their main business of minnow hunting. As I arrived at the lake-side I saw a really good trout head and tail within a long cast of the shallows. Getting down as low as possible, I put over him a large floating fly which I call "a shambles" (a rough dark brown hackle and a stiff ginger "whisker") and he took it at once with a good splashing rise. This was a very nice trout of one and three-quarter pounds.

Five minutes later I saw a bigger trout rise and got him too . . . two pounds, or just over. I then lost another of about one and a half pounds . . . and never saw another trout rise all day.

Changing my reel for an "Altex" I put on a small treble and a tiny bit of worm, and proceeded to foul-hook a minnow. In about two minutes this was accomplished, and I cast gently, letting the foul-hooked minnow drop about fifteen yards out in the deep.

Instantly I was taken by a trout that dived away

with a great rush, and after a minute or two had out a grand trout of just two pounds. Twice more I carried out this foul-hooking and casting routine, and each time hooked trout—both of which I lost.

Incidentally, one is apt to lose a lot of the fish that take one at this form of minnow fishing, because the trout does not always get the hook into his mouth, but only seizes the minnow.

I might have got a few more of these good trout that day, but I had to hurry home for some appointment.

Still, it had not been such a bad hour's fishing— three trout weighing five and three-quarter pounds, in a lake which is supposed to be a really dour fishing lake, and where the average is supposed to be about half a pound.

Of course, on a definitely "dour" lake the occasional really good hour or two's fishing which can be had now and then is not by any means typical.

Nevertheless, I found that by studying the trout and their little ways in this and other lakes, and by using a floating fly over rising fish, when the occasion arose, and then switching over to the live-minnow technique when they stopped rising, I got quite a nice lot of really big trout during July.

Apart from the "beetle" period in June, I had very few fish on these lynns except in July. In September I had an odd nice trout on a small devon-cast about thirty-five to forty yards down wind, and fished very slowly, i.e. deeply, back again.

This live-minnow method of fishing can be great fun in certain rivers, where the minnows congregate in late June or July, and the big chub and any trout that are there have a fortnight or more of concentrated feeding.

For many years, at a certain spot on the lower

Swale in Yorkshire, near my old home, I had the most wonderful chub fishing by this live-minnow method. I used to stand on a small bank of silt which had gradually formed into a tiny, reedy island, just above a certain bridge, and fish out into the deep water between this island and the bridge itself. Between the island and the shore thousands of minnows used to cluster in the shallow water—keeping out of the way of the big chub, I imagine, who cruised about in the deep, usually in full view of me. Every time I foul-hooked a minnow and swung it out into the deep water I had a chub at me.

One sunny day I remember well, as I caught a dozen chub—all good ones—from four pounds down to one and a half pounds, in half an hour or so. To round off the bag I had two trout—one of them one and a half pounds, which was good for that part of the Swale.

I think that anyone who hasn't tried this method, both for trout and the honest chevern, will agree with me when they do that there is no nicer fishing on a hot, still day, with the swallows diving over the surface of a clear, green river, or the cock grouse calling from the moor beyond some high lynn in Wales. . . .

You catch big fish on the lightest of tackle, and it is high summer—what more could a fisherman want?

CHAPTER VI

NATURAL-FLY FISHING

IT seems to me that in the absorbing and delightful cult of the artificial fly for the catching of trout and grayling, we have rather lost sight of the cult which formed the basis of all modern fly-fishing—the art of fishing with the natural insect.

At the period when Charles Cotton and Izaak Walton were catching fish and writing so charmingly about angling, fishermen were just beginning to make and use artificial flies, although most of them must still have been in the habit of using the natural fly on most occasions.

As far as one can discover, the general methods used by our ancestors in fishing the natural fly resembled somewhat the present-day method of dapping on the loughs of Eire, and in other places. Charles Cotton, although he made and used very tiny artificial flies, also fished with the natural. . . . He evidently used a rather long whippy rod, and probably a very long cast of horse-hair. The cast was tapered from a three-hair thickness to a point of a single hair. His remark about liking a "whistling wind" for his fishing is easily understood by anyone who has also fished the natural fly on a river, or, of course, on a lough.

Most people have at one time or another done a little "dibbling" with, say, a bluebottle on uncleared small rivers or brooks, but very few people seem to use

Robert M. Adam

THE WILDS OF GALLOWAY.   VIEW OF THE RIVER MINNOCH, NEAR BARGRENNAN

RUTHERFORD WATER—"THE CAULD"

MERTOUN WATER, LOOKING FROM THE TOP OF THE
"WILLOW BUSH" UP TO THE "HOUSE STREAM"

a natural fly on ordinary open rivers. I suppose one of the main reasons of this is the trouble and sometimes difficulty in catching a supply of suitable insects. Also, I think there is a general belief that one cannot *cast* with a natural fly, and that half a gale of wind is necessary to one's fishing. This is a quite unfounded belief. With a little care one can cast a reasonably long line using, say, a "daddy-long-legs", a bracken-clock beetle or a bluebottle. A grasshopper is also an insect which can be cast quite successfully.

In this sort of casting it is essential not to flick the fly too hard, and to be sure that it is fully extended behind before beginning the forward cast.

Apart from using a natural fly on the ordinary fly-fishing outfit, with, of course, a tiny plain hook taking the place of the artificial, it is possible to have great fun on, say, a ford of Tweed or any wide open stretch of river, if there is a good wind—preferably blowing upstream, or across and up—by using an ordinary thread-reel and two-pound B.st undressed silk line and a 5X cast.

The method here is, of course, simply to allow the natural insect to float out in front of one with the rod held rather high, and then to lower the rod point until the fly drops gently on to the stream.

With a little practice it is perfectly easy to keep "dapping" a "daddy", for example, over any likely spot, such as the "dead" water immediately downstream of a rock, or big stone. It is an amusing way of fishing, and I have always thought that one catches trout of a bigger average than with the artificial fly.

There are certain lochs in Scotland and lakes in other places which seem to be quite hopeless for ordinary wet-fly fishing under ordinary circumstances. It is on these sorts of lochs that I have found this

D

natural insect fishing to be a good and sometimes the
only way of having any sort of sport.

There are many lynns in Wales where the local
fishermen kill tremendous baskets of trout during the
few weeks of the "beetle" hatch. This "beetle" is, of
course, the small green beetle that appears on the
bracken in June, and is generally known as the bracken-
clock beetle.

This beetle can be cast quite as well as a natural fly,
and is infinitely better than the artificial "coch-y-
bondu" which imitates it. I have caught plenty of
trout on many of these dour hill lochs and lynns, with
various sorts of natural insect, when the artificial fly
was quite useless. "Daddy-long-legs", bracken-clock
beetles, ordinary black beetles from under stones, etc.,
grasshoppers and large sedges are all quite good for
this purpose. Of course, on many north-country rivers
the natural stone fly or its larvae ha been used from
time immemorial by the local fishers, with murderous
effect.

I once lived on a large reservoir, the water supply of
a great city. It had become, in fact, a very charming,
quite natural-looking lake, and had been stocked with
trout. I believe the trout fishing was very good for
quite a number of years, and then began, as is often
the case, to deteriorate.

When I arrived in the neighbourhood, the fishing
had become so fruitless that hardly a ticket was sold
during the season. Even the local inhabitants, who,
rightly or wrongly, fished when they felt inclined, with
or without a ticket, hardly ever caught anything but a
few small perch, and very occasionally a large trout.

To be precise, I had taken the house on this lake
because I had seen one of those trout! A magnificent
deep, small-headed three-pounder—caught on a night

line! I had some of the most pleasant fishing for a
few years using a small canoe. I rarely, if ever, caught
a trout during daylight, but used to fish a natural
sedge from about ten-thirty until twelve, and had some
really delightful sport with trout up to three and a half
pounds.

Those big trout never seemed to rise in the ordinary
way, but to confine themselves almost entirely to
cruising close to the surface after dark, and feeding on
the literally "giant" sedges which hatched out in the
reeds, and then could be seen "feathering" out on to
the lake's surface.

Fishing on this lake was utterly useless on windy,
wet or cold nights. Unfortunately, these nights were
the rule, and not the exception.

In practice there are all sorts of ways of fishing in
this way, and I have always found it a most interesting
type of fishing. The main thing to remember is that
one is fishing with a natural fly, and that it is better
to be really slow about striking; there is very little
chance that a trout will drop the fly immediately after
taking it, as so often happens with an artificial.

I intend to try this natural-fly technique on Blagdon
this summer; I have an idea it may be very killing. One
of the big Blagdon trout on a light rod and a 2 lb. B.S.
line would be rather an experience.

CHAPTER VII

FISHING WITH A RUBBER DINGHY

IT is rather surprising that so little notice has been taken of the advent into the fishing world of the cheap rubber dinghy. Thousands upon thousands of these little boats of various sizes are being offered for sale from Government surplus stocks, at amazingly cheap prices; and yet I meet very few fishermen who have thought of using them. Thousands of these little rubber coracles are being bought by bathing enthusiasts and seaside holiday-makers. More thousands are being bought for children to play about in—but comparatively few are, as yet, used by fishermen.

Personally, I think these dinghies will very soon be looked upon as part of an angler's outfit, just as much as a landing net or a fishing bag is now.

In the spring of 1947 I became the proud owner, for the sum of fifty shillings, of one of these dinghies. It arrived by parcel-post. The parcel contained the boat itself, a mast (telescopic), a beautiful bright red sail, a cross-strut to support the sail and two small rubber paddles. There was also a tiny inflating gadget which fitted into a little pocket in the side of one of the bulk-heads—a really amazing fifty-shillings' worth!

An astonishingly dry and hot summer on the west coast of Argyll afforded me plenty of opportunities of getting accustomed to my new toy. On the whole,

I do not think I have bought anything for years which has given me such amusement. . . .

Experience taught me one or two useful additions to the outfit, and also that I had very little use for the beautiful bright red sail. When there was enough wind on our sea-loch to make the sail usable, the swell and choppy sea made the dinghy a remarkably alarming and rather wet craft.

The astonishing thing is that one instinctively thinks at first that one is going to upset at any moment, but in fact one just can't upset. All that can happen is that the dinghy fills with water—very easily—and one finds oneself sitting in a kind of hip-bath, still merrily sailing or paddling along. A great advance on the bowl used by the honest men of Gotham, but still rather uncomfortable.

However, the real use and beauty of the dinghy is found to be in fresh water, on rivers of all sorts, even burns, and above all on lochs. All through the amazing summer of 1947 I visited numbers of hill lochs and lochans. Places on which no boat had even floated in living memory. Lochs to which it would be next to impossible to take a boat by any means.

The whole outfit went very nicely into a good-sized game bag, together with a square plywood board (a very useful addition) to sit on, a fifteen- or twenty-yard length of strong cord and one rubber ground-sheet.

After arriving at the selected loch, I unpacked the contents of my game bag, inflated the dinghy (in about five minutes) with its own bellows, placed in it the ply-wood board, and on top of the board the ground-sheet, folded into a square cushion, and on top of the ground-sheet the game bag itself. To one of the straps on one of the bulkheads I fastened my strong cord, to the end of which I tied a suitable stone, and coiled it ready for use on the little "deck" formed at the bow by the oilskin cover, or apron, which was, by the way, one of the features of the little boat.

I then placed my rod ready for use with the point sticking out over the bow of the dinghy (a seven- or eight-foot rod is best for this exercise), a small landing net then followed, placed so that the net-head hung out over the side.

All being more or less ready, I then half lifted and half dragged my boat down to the loch side, walked out, still dragging it, for about four yards into the loch (in gum-boots), and then, when the dinghy was floating in about one foot or one and a half feet of water, proceeded to get in and make myself comfortable.

The two small paddles, meanwhile, were wedged, one at each bulkhead, under loops which were really meant for use in carrying the boat.

I found that this little dingy (there are larger ones to be bought, of course) was perfectly navigable by means of the two toy-like rubber paddles, and that I could move along even against a slight breeze quite easily. One could also go backwards or forwards with equal ease.

The first time I fished out of my new boat was on a small lochan, a sort of minor appendage of a much larger loch, a lochan almost choked with water-lilies and completely unfishable from the banks. Right out in the middle of the lily-pads was a space of open water, about a quarter of an acre in extent, in which I had often seen really good trout rising.

On this first occasion I propelled myself with about three strokes of the paddles through or over the water-lilies, and then placing myself in the middle of the open water, dropped my stone gently over the side, as an anchor, and was ready for anything.

Being so low in the water, the passage of this little craft does not seem to disturb trout at all, and I imagine it is much less noisy than even the most skilfully handled boat of the usual type.

A good trout rose within five yards of me, and I put a floating tup over him. This trout was hooked at once, and as he turned out to be a very large trout for that small loch, just over one pound, he pulled the light dinghy about from side to side in the most amazing manner. If I had not put down my anchor he would definitely have towed me all over the open water.

Incidentally, I have often been towed about by a two-pound trout, in a canoe. On this, my first trial voyage in my tiny boat, I had four extremely nice trout within half an hour, and learned quite a lot about what to do and not to do when a trout has been hooked under these circumstances.

The whole thing was amazingly interesting, and instructive. Firstly, it is very fascinating to feel that one is fishing in a place that has never been cast over before, and to hook trout that could never by any means have been reached in any other way.

Secondly, one is so close to the water, actually in the water, that it is, at first, quite a novel experience playing a fish that is splashing or jumping almost on a level with one's shoulders.

Later the same day I carried the dinghy over about half a mile of moor to float it on the large loch. Here there was a slight breeze, and I managed to do quite respectable "drifts" with the help of a light stone substituted for the anchor stone I had on the cord at first.

On this first occasion I had not thought of the technique of the plywood board, the ground-sheet and the game bag used as a seat, and was just sitting right down on the bottom of the boat.

This, I found, was apt to be rather chilly work as there was nothing between oneself and the waters of the loch but a little thin rubber!

I also gave myself quite a shock by touching—with my latter end—a submerged rock which I hadn't known about. For an instant I had a horrible idea that some monster trout had "risen" at a new sort of water-beetle. Then I realized what had caused the hump, and that sitting as I was on the rubber bottom of the dinghy I was making myself into a kind of keel that protruded about two feet below the rest of the dinghy. From this, of course, evolved the idea of the plywood board as a seat.

The uses in fishing of these little rubber boats seem to me to be almost endless. One can fish lochs that would be totally unfishable under ordinary circumstances; reach casts on big rivers on which there are no available boats, especially places where a fast "run" goes out into a big pool, places where the salmon always seem to lie right out far beyond the longest cast, at the very tail of these "runs".

I can also think of many places where the sea trout rise at night, certain places in Wales and elsewhere, that are quite unfishable in the ordinary way. These places would be quite easily fished in a rubber dinghy.

The coracle fisher has, of course, always known the uses of such boats, but then few people have much enthusiasm for fishing out of a coracle on swirling, deep salmon rivers.

The rubber dinghy has all the advantages and none of the drawbacks of a coracle. It is also very much easier to carry.

I hope this summer to find many more uses for my little toy boat. I have still a great treat in store in this respect; to hook and kill a salmon in a big, fast river. All sorts of things may happen—but it will be a great experience.

CHAPTER VIII

SOME SUGGESTIONS ON
WHERE TO FISH

DESPITE the periodic appearance of fishing guides, gazetteers and pamphlets about "Where to Fish", I think most fishermen will agree with me that nothing very satisfactory in this respect has been produced in this country, with the notable exception of *The Field*'s *Where to Fish* edited in 1939 and before by Mr. Turing, and now in the new edition, by Mr. Luscombe.

Even this excellent book, which I and many other fishers have, for years, looked upon almost as our "bible", fails, probably through its own comprehensiveness, to give the tourist-angler any real idea of the type of river to be fished, and its "atmosphere".

In trying to give a novice fisherman some idea of where to fish, I shall merely outline a few places where I myself, or where my friends, have fished. I think it better to be brief and accurate than long-winded and inaccurate. I think the best way to attempt this is to deal with each month of the fishing year in turn, for, to anyone who has spent a lifetime looking for and trying new rivers, each month does indeed carry its own mental picture of fishings and methods of fishing.

February, for instance, has its own bare and frigid atmosphere; as bald and windswept as North Wark or

Sprouston-on-Tweed, and as steely-blue and beautiful as a fresh-run twenty-pounder.

March again, in its earlier part, is much the same as February, while all its later days have about them the eternally renewed atmosphere of spring and March browns and rising trout.

And so it is with each month of the year. . . . Even December and January have their own peculiar mental "scent" of frost-stiffened reeds and the wide tail of a pike that has just slashed at a "wagtail" or a spun dace.

Let us consider, therefore, a few of the pleasant places that we may visit for the catching of trout from March until September.

*   *   *   *   *

Without the least hesitation I would name the Tweed as the most varied and still one of the most productive of all our rivers.

There are any amount of places to stay all down Tweed, from Peebles to Norham, but personally I would make for Coldstream or Cornhill. If you want to fish in Scotland, stay in Coldstream, if in England, Cornhill.

There is a Lower Tweed tradition that lays down the rule that if you are fishing with your back to England you are fishing in England; if with Scotland at your back, Scotland. The trout of Crooky, Milnegraden or Ladykirk don't mind a bit. . . .

One of the most delightful places to stay in these parts is the Tillmouth Castle Hotel, which stands over the lower Till not many hundreds of yards from where that lovely little river flows into Tweed.

Incidentally, just below this junction is one of

the most famous salmon casts—the Pot Point stream.

If the fisherman stays at Tillmouth, he will not only be comfortable, and well-treated, but will have what is probably the best all-round trout fishing in the North within easy walking distance.

Near the mouth of the Till, on the Cornhill bank of the Tweed, used to stand a tiny chapel, which gave its name to the famous chapel-stream cast, which is now, alas, ruined by silting gravel-beds.

This chapel, one autumn night just over 400 years ago, was crowded with wounded men who had crawled there for sanctuary; wreckage of the fatal battle that had been lost and won a few miles away below Flodden Hill. . . .

But nowadays, whether you prefer to fish a wet-fly down the wide rippling "fords" when the icy wind from Berwick mingles the snow-flakes and the March browns, or to try a dry greenwell upstream, there is no place where you are more likely to fill a creel.

There are also innumerable places which are quite perfect for the spinning of a small natural minnow.

In fact, it was hereabouts that many years ago I first saw the thread-line technique being used extensively.

If the visitor finds that Tillmouth is a little too far off the beaten track for his purposes, the famous Collingwood Arms at Cornhill is at his disposal. Here he will find the atmosphere of a really old and well-seasoned fishing inn which was and still is the real headquarters of a very secretive and perfectly organized coterie of true salmon fishers, who for the past seventy or more years have dealt with uncountable spring and autumn salmon between the Willow Pool and Twizell. . . .

The trout fishing of Tweed is entirely free, and one

can fish anywhere, except on the well-known and recognized salmon pools and casts, which, incidentally, are for the most part quite unsuited to the trout fishermen.

Although much despised, as I think wrongly, by the local fishers, the grayling fishing in Tweed is remarkably good in October and November. . . .

The local fishermen will tell you amazing tales of the great catches of trout taken in Tweed "in the old days", but I doubt if the fishing has deteriorated much in a hundred years.

Mr. Alexander Wanless once made some very interesting researches into this question. He found that many records had been kept over a century or more by several fishing associations. These records proved what many of us had suspected. Our grandfathers and great-grandfathers did indeed catch enormous *numbers* of trout, but the surprising fact emerged, from a study of the actual records, that the average weight of trout caught was barely three ounces!

Considering that the Tweed trout, even in these "degenerate" days, average reasonably well, one receives the inescapable impression that our hardy ancestors were in the habit of taking whole creels full of *salmon parr*!

Be that as it may, anyone who really loves trout fishing on a great river in beautiful surroundings could not do better than spend the month of March on Tweed.

In April, the Border rivers are also very good, but then so are some rivers further north. In South Wales or in Devonshire, April is also a most delightful fishing month.

In the north-east of Scotland, such rivers as the Don and Deveron and the little rivers of Bogie and Isla can

be very well worth fishing. The hotel at Alford Bridge
on the Don is one of the very best centres for trout
fishing, and the Gordon Arms or Huntley Arms at
Huntley for fishing the Deveron, the Bogie and the
Isla, are both very comfortable indeed, and quite close
to the fishing.

The Bogie is an absolutely perfect small river to fish
with a floating fly; the only trouble is that the trout
are very small. One can wade in ordinary stocking
waders or thigh boots right up the middle of this little
river, and it is the greatest fun possible to cast a large
tup or greenwell or any large-hackled fly upstream
over rising trout.

I once had fifteen brace of nice small trout from the
Bogie between ten o'clock and lunch time.

The Usk at Crickhowell, in South Wales, is another
place where the trout fishing is excellent in April and
May. Here the trout are of a good average weight,
and it is quite possible to get three or four brace of fish
averaging over half a pound on either a wet-fly or dry,
when conditions are anything like suitable. The hotel
at Crickhowell is very comfortable, and is used to
catering for fishermen. The Usk fishing is not as good
as formerly, through neglect during the War, but will
improve.

For small trout in April nowhere could be nicer
fishing than the moorland streams of Devonshire, and
one of the best ways of spending a holiday is to stay
at Dulverton or Simonsbath, and divide one's time
between hunting and fishing.

There are plenty of very comfortable hotels to stay
at where one can always hire a good horse for a day
with the stag hounds. The fishing in the Barle and
Exe has a peculiar charm of its own.

Although the fishing is not really very good, and the

trout rather small, this Devonshire moorland fishing has a definite "atmosphere" which exercises an extraordinary fascination for many fishermen, especially in the spring time, which is much the best time of the year in the West Country.

In May, the best of the North Country trout fishing is over, except in the chalk streams of East Yorkshire, where it is only just beginning.

Dry-fly fishing in the Derwent, Driffield Beck and Foston Beck is not too easy to get for the casual fisherman, but many of the landowners who have fishing and some of the fishing clubs will, on occasions, grant permission to visitors.

The fishing in the Driffield Beck, the Foston Beck and several other chalk streams can be absolutely first-class. The dry-fly fishing, particularly in the Mayfly season, on the Driffield Club water or the Foston Beck almost approaches the semi-religious eminence of Stockbridge or Leckford on the Test.

Moving further south, the lovely little rivers of the Cotswolds are quite delightful, although there is, nowadays, some pollution and the fishing is nothing like as good as it should be.

The best centre for fishing the Cotswold rivers is, I think, Fairford on the Colne. Here, at the Bull Hotel, one can really try out one's skill with a dry-fly, and also one's pretensions to be a true fisher.

The Colne at Fairford is a quite perfect dry-fly stream, and there are some good trout to be seen and fished over, but their standard of education is almost incredibly high. It is so high that on many occasions wise and patient fishermen of forty years' experience have been known to assert that the trout are uncatchable! This, of course, is not so, but these Colne trout are remarkably intelligent.

Unfortunately nearly all the Cotswold rivers have been much neglected during the War. The Colne and several other rivers are very badly weeded up. There is also some evidence of pollution by milk " washings ".

There is fishing to be had, either through various clubs or from the landowners, on most of these Cotswold streams. Apart entirely from the catching of trout there is no more lovely country in the world than these little river valleys that feed the Thames. It is a magic country indeed in May, and it is a very lovely thing to walk back to one's hotel on some quiet evening from the river—at Fairford, or Lechlade, although in these days you will probably have caught no more than a brace of smallish trout. And then, after the small clear streams of the Cotswold valleys, I would suggest a short journey to Blagdon for a fishing holiday of quite another sort.

This Blagdon fishing for big rainbows and brown trout is a very different thing from loch-fishing in Scotland, or the North of England. Here, the ordinary technique of drifting and fishing with three or more sunken flies is of little practical use. Except sometimes on still nights, there is rarely any real movement of trout which might be called a rise, and the trolling of a minnow in those parts of the lake where this is allowed is apt to be disappointing.

Most Blagdon fishers use large, brightly-coloured sea-trout flies or lures, fished very deep in the water, and very slowly, the whole process being more like salmon fishing on Loch Lomond or Loch Maree than ordinary trout fishing.

Incidentally, it is not at all impossible to find oneself suddenly attached to a trout as big as a smallish salmon; a trout too which will fight much more savagely than most salmon.

FIONN LOCH, VIEW FROM THE NORTH WITH BEINN AIRIDH CHARR ON RIGHT

Robert M. Adam

LOCH EADAR DHA, WITH CAMAS UIG IN DISTANCE, ISLE OF LEWIS

During the war, when no boat-fishing was allowed on Blagdon, many people developed the practice of wading and found that in many ways it was better than the time-honoured reliance on a boat.

I think Blagdon an ideal place to practice the natural-fly technique, which I mentioned in an earlier chapter. The way to do this, as on most Scottish lochs, is to wade out over one of the many gravelly shallows when the wind is blowing in one's face, and then, turning round, cast a live sedge or grasshopper down the wind *towards* the shore. If you can see a big fish move, which sometimes happens, on still evenings, and you can get a natural fly anywhere near him, you will be in for a few minutes of real excitement.

A five- or six-pound trout on a 4X cast must be treated with respect and on Blagdon it is very essential to have plenty of "backing" on your reel. A big rainbow when hooked nearly always makes for deep water, and may run you out anything up to a hundred or more yards of line; if you are wading, you will not be able to follow him, of course.

This Blagdon fishing, and, for that matter, the fishing on nearly all big "made" lakes, is not everybody's sort of fishing, but the catching of the really big trout of Blagdon is definitely an art in itself, and well worth the while of any keen trout fisherman.

*　　*　　*　　*　　*

The month of June is without question the "sweet of the year" as far as trout fishing in Southern England is concerned. The only drawback from a casual fisherman's point of view is that almost everybody is well aware of this fact, and it is correspondingly hard to find anywhere to fish.

E

However, there is at least one place where it is
possible to enjoy really first-class dry-fly fishing
if one is prepared or able to pay for it. Lord
Normanton's fishery near Ringwood is well worth a
visit.

Here is a very carefully keepered fishing where, for
about £2 2s. a day, one may see and fish for really
"warrantable" trout. The trout are, in fact, all or
nearly all "stew" trout, i.e. hatchery trout which are
turned into the water when they reach about one and
a half pounds in weight. I have heard remarks about
these "stew" trout being tame, and not to be compared with "wild" trout. . . . Personally, I cannot
agree about "stew" trout being in any way inferior
or different from so-called "wild" ones. My own
experience of stocking has taught me that a trout
reared and fed in stew-ponds up to any weight does,
in fact, become extremely "wild" after he has been at
liberty for some months, and fished over.

Of course, if you fish for trout when they are first
turned into a fishery, straight from the hatchery, they
are naturally very unsophisticated, and will take *anything* thrown on to the water . . . *but* they very soon
become educated. . . . As for their fighting qualities,
a two-pound trout, fresh from a stew pond, will fight
every bit as well as a trout which has been born and
bred in a river.

In any case, this Avon fishery at Ringwood is quite
first-class in many ways, and is one of the very few
places where outsiders have a chance of really good
chalk-stream fishing.

It used to be possible to fish the famous Leckford
water, near Stockbridge, by ticket, but nowaday's
this is not so. However, if some kind friend is good
enough to give you a day, you will find the fishing

quite exceptionally good and most perfectly looked after.

If one cannot manage to be in Hampshire during June, I cannot think of any better substitute than the Peacock, at Rowsley, in Derbyshire, an extremely comfortable hotel, which has a number of rods for its visitors on the Haddon Hall fishery of the Wye, and fishing rights in the Derwent.

This Wye fishing is quite unique, as far as English trout fishing is concerned, as this is one of the very few rivers in this country where the rainbow has done well.

The only fault to be found with this lovely few miles of fishing on the beautiful Haddon Hall estate is that the rainbows have done *too well*. These bright and lively aliens have, within thirty years, managed to wipe out the original population of brown trout, which in many ways is a great pity. This Haddon Hall fishing was, once upon a time, one of the very best dry-fly fishings in England. Nowadays, one rarely sees a brown trout.

Curiously enough, the grayling seem to have thriven exceedingly alongside the rainbows—despite the most intensive netting.

In any case, here is a most delightful place to fish, in an "atmosphere" which cannot be surpassed from a true fisherman's point of view. The Wye is a most delightful little river, and there is no better place for seeing trout and for trying out all one's skill in approach and presentation of a fly.

The catching of small rainbows of three-quarters of a pound or less is all too easy; to return to the Peacock with a brace or so of trout above one and a half pounds the work of a master.

The big rainbows, of which there are plenty, do not rise well to a floating fly, but can often be lured by a really cunningly placed nymph. There is, I am certain, no better place for a novice to acquire experience than on this lovely "rainbow river" of the Derbyshire Wye.

If one stays at the Peacock or the Rutland Arms at Bakewell, one can also fish the Derwent between Baslow and Matlock. In this length of river, despite the menace of a certain number of coarse fish, there are very good brown trout to be caught, and it is a lovely river to fish.

While in the neighbourhood, a visitor would be well advised to stay for a few days at the Izaak Walton Hotel in Dovedale, to fish the very own little river of Charles Cotton and the old "master" Walton himself.

The Izaak Walton fishing of the Dove and the Manifold is essentially "dale" fishing, where the trout are small, but the whole atmosphere of the district is so charming that the size of the trout caught is a very secondary matter.

From July onwards I would suggest that my imaginary trout-fisher should leave England and the English summer behind and go north—and keep going north. It seems to me that during July, August and September the trout-fisher would be well advised to devote his time to the theory and practice of loch fishing, and that most fascinating pastime of burn fishing.

To really enjoy loch fishing at its best there can be no argument that a car is very helpful, if not absolutely necessary. Not only does a car enable one to fish many more lochs and burns than if one is forced to walk or hire a conveyance, but it also acts as a kind of movable fishing hut.

To my mind one of the few really unpleasant features of fishing out-of-the-way lochs is the frequency with which one finds oneself a somewhat forlorn little figure in a very large and forbidding landscape; a figure that can be and often is entirely without shelter from wind or rain, and a very long way from home!

The ideal loch is one where a car can be driven right up to the lochside, even if this means a slow and shattering progress up a so-called road which is in reality a small river-bed. If one can get a car right to the edge of the loch, there is no form of fishing more pleasant than this.

On the vast majority of good fishing lochs, a boat of some sort is provided. If there is no boat, a rubber dinghy, as mentioned in an earlier chapter, is a good substitute.

Now as to where to fish. It would, of course, need a whole book, and a long one at that, to answer this query, even as far as the west and north of Scotland is concerned, so I will mention just a few places which I have either fished myself, or know about through fishing friends.

It has always seemed to me that one of the definite capitals, as it were, of loch fishing, is Lairg in Sutherland, at the southern end of Loch Shin. There is not a great deal of good fishing, as far as trout are concerned, at Lairg itself, but from here one can reach all sorts of delightful places—some famous, some almost unknown. There are various services of motor-coaches from Lairg to such places as Inchnadamph, Invershin, Altnacealgach Hotel, Scourie, Bettyhill Hotel and Altnaharra Hotel.

If you are without a car of your own, I would suggest going direct to, say, Scourie or Bettyhill, which are places where almost endless loch fishing, burn fishing, and estuary fishing can be enjoyed.

Round about Scourie are at least a hundred lochs, many of them very good indeed. The hotel is excellent.

If you go to the Altnacealgach Hotel, you can fish very many lochs, among them the very excellent brown trout lochs of Urigill and Veyatie.

If you go up to Bettyhill or Durness or the Kyle of Tongue, you can, of course, get the very best of sea-trout fishing both in fresh and salt water, and some salmon fishing besides a very delightful variety of different types of trout fishing.

The big hotel at Gairloch on the coast of Ross, not far from Loch Maree, is remarkably comfortable, and they have some really excellent lochs within a radius of a few miles.

In good weather, which, by the way, is not so unusual as many people seem to think in the North-West Highlands, Gairloch is a most perfect place for a holiday. There are very good stretches of sand and the bathing is almost perfect. This corner of North-West Scotland is particularly favoured by our old school-friend the Gulf Stream, and it often comes as quite a surprise to southern visitors to discover that after travelling about 700 miles northwards from London they are in a more or less sub-tropical climate where all sorts of foreign trees and shrubs can survive.

As far as loch fishing is concerned, one might fish in this north-west area every summer for a life-time and still find that there are dozens of lochs which one has never even visited.

Once, looking out over Ross-shire from the screes of Ben Slioch above Loch Maree I counted thirty or more different lochs—all within about a radius of ten miles. Here, behind Ben Slioch, is one of the very perfect brown-trout lochs of Scotland—the Fionn Loch. I believe this loch can now be fished, on occasions from the Poolewe Hotel. The average size of the trout in this loch is really remarkable.

Any true and honest fisher who happens to find himself at the tiny village of Poolewe, at the Loch Ewe end of the Ewe River would be well advised to inquire from the hotel about this fishing. There are also some good lochs which can be fished from Poolewe.

If one has had enough of Scottish fishing by the end of August, September is a very good month for fishing many rivers further south. In North Yorkshire there are a number of rivers where the trout fishing, while very much like the Tweed and other Border rivers, in many ways, are rather smaller and more easily fished.

The Yore from Ripon right up to Aysgarth, is one of the loveliest rivers in Britain. At Tanfield most of the water is preserved, stocked and keepered by a very progressive club, but I believe that tickets can be procured on occasions. The water bailiff at Tanfield, who is also in charge of a hatchery, or Mr. Hodgson, tackle dealer and gunsmith in Ripon, would give all up-to-date particulars.

The Upper Swale, from Catterick right up Swaledale, is remarkably pleasant fishing, and the trout, for so cold a river, average very well. The Swale between Richmond and Reeth is one of the most beautiful few miles of river imaginable, and is well worth fishing, either with a fly or minnow.

It seems to me that when my imaginary fisherman has fished the few places I have mentioned, and tried out a few or all of the methods suggested, he will have reached the conclusion that Britain still has a certain amount of trout fishing left for all honest men and fishermen, whether they are rich or poor.

PART II

ON THE CATCHING OF SALMON

CHAPTER IX

SPRING FISHING WITH FLY AND BAIT

THERE have been countless books written as to what
salmon take, why they take it, and how to catch them.
Recently the fashion appears to have been to infer that
they are quite easy to catch if one only knows *how* to
catch them. One writer in recent years has even gone
so far as to state that he believes the hooking of salmon
is 95 per cent skill and only 5 per cent luck. Personally,
I am so humble or stupid as to believe that exactly the
contrary is the case. However, like "old Khayyam",
having listened all my life to numberless "doctors"
(frequently from Harley Street) and a few "saints"
arguing "about it and about", I have always gone out
by the "same door as in I went. . . ."

The best explanation of the unexplainable vagaries
of the honest Salar I have heard is that the taking of a
fly or bait is a kind of mental aberration; a type of
insanity or may be just a gesture of absent-mindedness.

However, the fact remains that salmon do take
quite heartily on plenty of occasions, and that a very
great number are hooked and landed each year, to
the delight of numberless fishermen.

One of the few stable factors in the whole exercise is that undoubtedly *fresh*-run fish do take better than fish that have been for some time in fresh water. This, I think, gives some weight to the suggestion that a salmon, when it slashes at a fly or a golden sprat, is acting in a careless and absent-minded way, remembering perhaps, his voracious feeding habits in the sea. The longer he has been away from salt water, the fainter grows this memory, hence the "dourness" of stale fish.

When advising a beginner about the catching of salmon, I should like to point out that in salmon fishing in Great Britain, the best single object in a would-be fisherman's outfit is undoubtedly a really active and usable cheque-book. This is not to say that a poor man cannot catch a great many salmon, but unquestionably a rich man who is also a keen fisherman has a very much better chance of catching more. For this reason I do not consider salmon fishing, as a sport, compares with trout fishing, or even some types of coarse fishing.

I think that the first thing to be realized about salmon fishing is that, generally speaking, it is divided fairly clearly into three parts: spring fishing, summer fishing, and autumn fishing. Of these, the first is certainly the most productive, the second the most sporting, and the third the most uncertain and disappointing.

Although spring salmon fishing has the name of being a most expensive sport, it is quite possible for spring fish to be caught at a comparatively moderate cost.

The famous fishings of the Tweed and Scottish or Welsh Dee, the best beats of the Wye or Spey are, quite truly, astonishingly expensive, and are, in any case, very difficult to lease. And yet, the curious fact has become clear in recent years, through the very high price of salmon, that more often than not the more one pays for a beat on a good spring fishing, the less one is ultimately out of pocket, which remark would appear a trifle "Irish" until one examines the matter in detail.

Supposing one takes a famous beat of the Dee or Tweed for the three or four best months, i.e., February, March, April and May, it is not at all unlikely that five hundred or even six hundred fish will be killed on the water during that time.

If these fish are sold at about five shillings per pound, and the average is, say, ten pounds, it will be seen that at any rent of less than £1,200 the fishing will have cost the tenant little or nothing.

It is a gamble, like any other commercial transaction, which may or may not come off.

The most expensive salmon fishing, of course, is a poor, uncertain fishing, which produces few fish.

However, as all this sounds much more like some business transaction than a sport which, unfortunately, is the case where "good" salmon fishing is concerned, we will content ourselves for a time with a few methods of procedure which may be of interest to novices in a great and royal pastime.

To begin with, the question of tackle immediately arises.

I have noticed that many books on salmon fishing, when this question of rods and tackle occurs, recommend the beginner to buy only "the best". Now to my mind, this advice, while being many ways quite correct, is somewhat ambiguous and fraught with financial dangers. The novice who surrenders to some eminent tackle-manufacturer, and, as they say "puts himself in their hands" must also be prepared to put anything up to £200 "in their hands . . .".

The whole matter is rather in the same category as the expensive novitiate of the would-be game-shot who starts by having a pair of guns made for him by some famous firm of gun-smiths. By the time he has had his eyes tested, his guns fitted and re-fitted and has fired off perhaps a thousand cartridges at a shooting-school, the late but inevitable arrival of his bill may well surprise him.

And, in the end, he may find that he is no better shot than some impoverished friend, who uses a £15 or £20 gun, has not the faintest idea which "eye is the master", and who has never fired a shot at a shooting-school in his life.

On the other hand, in salmon fishing, like every other branch of sport, it *is* essential to have the correct tackle, correct in the utility sense, and not the social.

For fly-fishing for salmon, I am convinced that greenheart rods are infinitely preferable to split-cane, and that a spliced rod is infinitely better than a ferruled rod.

If one salmon fly rod only is required (which I think is in most cases so), I think that the novice could do no better than to buy a spliced "Grant Vibration" rod from Messrs. Playfair of Aberdeen. The length, for all-round use, should be thirteen feet, or perhaps thirteen feet six inches. A Hardy or a Leonard twelve-feet split cane is a lovely thing, but will not do what a "Vibration" greenheart will do, and will cost about three times as much.

Any sort of good, well-made reel which balances will do with this rod, but I would recommend the purchase of two casting lines—one of them rather heavy—the other rather on the light side. For early spring fishing or late autumn fishing, when it is necessary to get a big fly well down in the water, the heavy line is very useful. The lighter line is almost essential for so-called greased line fishing, and for all occasions when the water is getting warmer, and the fish to be fished near the surface.

The use of gut or nylon is a rather controversial point. Nylon is very cheap and has apparently no real faults, except that its stretching characteristic makes the tying of careful knots very essential, but there have been occasions when I have had doubts—grave doubts —about it. I do not know why it is, but I have lost more salmon through being broken during the three or four seasons I have been using nylon than during all the seasons when I used gut.

On the whole, I should advise the novice to be really extravagant about the buying of his casts, and in this case really have "nothing but the best" gut. It may be that the astonishing and unpredictable stresses and strains put upon a cast by a salmon while he is being played find out some obscure weakness in nylon about which neither the manufacturer nor the fisherman knows anything. Anyway, use gut and be sure, is my advice.

As for flies, I am certain that a very few patterns and three sizes are all that anyone requires. The buying of salmon flies can be a fantastically expensive amusement nowadays. As it is quite easy to learn how to tie and make your own, why go to this expense? When I say tie your own flies, I do not suggest that you should spend laborious, if happy, hours making delightful creations in imitation of the glorious and exotic confections which one sees on a tackle-dealer's tray. By no means. In my experience the noble Salar much

prefers a sad-looking, somewhat dimly-dressed object,
to the opulent-looking and gaudily-over-dressed aristocrats of the fly catalogues.

I have always found that a fly becomes more and
more deadly as it gets more and more ragged and
unkempt-looking. Therefore, why not start by using
flies which you, as a novice, have tied yourself? Your
very mistakes and fumblings will produce that degree
of dishevelment and shabbiness which salmon seem
to appreciate.

If the novice does not want to tie his own, I would
advise him to buy a few gold-ribbed March Browns,
as used largely on the Scottish Dee, a few Blue
Charms, a few Jock Scotts, and one or two Black
Doctors.

I think that three sizes of fly should suffice for almost
all occasions. A large two-inch fly for early spring
fishing, a medium-sized fly for the later spring, and a
small, very thinly-dressed one for greased-line fishing,
and all spring and autumn work in low water. I will
not waste much time on this subject, as I am unshak-
ably convinced that within reason it doesn't matter
one little bit what you use.

Recently I watched a friend of mine hook and land
three salmon within an hour, spinning good-sized
golden sprats (sprats of a size one would use on the
Tweed in March) in dead, low, gin-clear water in
which one could not only see the salmon, but almost
count their scales!

I myself had been fishing a greased-line over these
salmon, with a tiny low-water Blue Charm, without
having moved a single fish.

The main thing about all salmon fishing is to be
there, on the water, when, for some utterly unknown
reason, the fish take it into their heads to remember

the ravishing taste of herring fly, or, maybe, Mr. Waddington's elvers, during their sea-going days.

* * * * * *

One of the best ways to begin salmon fishing is to wangle, beg or buy a week or a fortnight on Tweed in February, March or April. The great fishings of Sprouston, Birgham, Wark and the rest may be extremely difficult of approach in this respect, but discreet inquiries from Messrs. Forrest, in Kelso or in the regions about Coldstream or Cornhill on Tweed, by any honest man who gives the impression of being a true fisher, sometimes bear fruit.

After the end of May, when the spring fishing is considered to be over, it is often possible to get a few days or even a fortnight at a reasonable cost on one of the really famous beats. To the greased-line fisher or the caster of a small shrimp or a small natural minnow with a thread-line reel, this fishing can be very good, although nearly all the fish caught will not be exactly fresh-run.

If the novice *can* manage to get a week or more in the early spring, he may, given normal luck, begin his salmon-fishing career in really heartening style.

Bearing out my previous remarks about the relative skill of salmon and trout fishing, I once knew a young man who had quite literally never fished before—even for a roach—who landed eight fresh-run fish on the Tweed in one day, and lost six others. He could be forgiven for thinking that salmon fishing was an almost childishly simple matter. I have no doubt that the passing years have taught him how wrong he was!

In the spinning of a large bait in spring, it is curious how the fishermen and boatmen on various rivers have their own convinced opinions about the relative merits of natural baits, such as sand-eels, golden or silver sprats, gudgeon etc., and artificial baits such as Devons, phantoms, spoons, etc.

On the Border rivers, and the Aberdeenshire Dee, it is considered absolutely essential to use only natural baits, while on many other rivers, such as the Exe, Wye, etc., the artificial bait is used almost exclusively. Personally, I have never really believed that it makes any difference, although I think it much better to follow the local customs in this respect.

On the whole, I believe a medium-sized golden sprat to be about the best all-round bait for "heavy" spring fishing. When using a thread-line reel and fine tackle in clear water, I have no doubt at all that a small natural minnow is the best bait of all.

Regarding spring bait fishing, there is, I think, very little that I can say, and nothing that a good boatman or ghillie will not tell the novice. The main thing to remember when spinning in cold, big water in the spring is that the salmon are very sluggish at this time, and the bait should be spun as slowly as possible, which means as deeply as possible. . . .

In May, when the water begins to warm up, a fly is usually much better than bait, always excepting the small minnow or spun shrimp used with a fixed-spool reel.

In any case, there is something extraordinarily fascinating about this spring salmon fishing. I have noticed on the Tweed that one often enjoys a week or two of almost summer-like weather in February or March. When this happens, and one is lucky enough to be fishing some famous beat between Kelso or Norham, one seems to touch for a time the very heart of spring.

Robert M. Adam

GRIMERSTA RIVER, ISLE OF LEWIS

MIDDLE BIRGHAM WATER, SHOWING "THE THREE STANES"
AND "PIKEY"

UPPER BIRGHAM WATER.   BOTTOM OF "WEIL STREAM"
SHOWING THE "WEIL ROCKS" ON THE OPPOSITE SIDE

The last fortnight of May can also be a fairy time when all the high woods are flecked with the gold of primroses, and sometimes the fresh-run fish rise like trout to a small fly fished almost on the surface.

CHAPTER X

THE ARTISTIC USE OF A
THREAD-LINE REEL FOR SALMON

IT is, I think, only a slight exaggeration to say that since the invention of the reel itself nothing has had such a profound influence on fishing as the development of the fixed-spool reel. It has opened up whole new vistas in the world of angling.

For myself, I feel that almost every season brings some new idea for experiment based on this priceless little device. For spinning light baits, either downstream, cross-stream, or upstream, it is admirably efficient; for shrimp and prawn fishing it has transformed a clumsy and heavy-handed type of fishing into something which is definitely as much an art as true dry-fly fishing. For worm fishing in all sorts and conditions of water it is supreme; for the technique of the upstream worm it is altogether delightful. In the world of coarse-fish angling its advent has been just as dramatic.

A great deal of our knowledge about this thread-line fishing and much of its popularity is undoubtedly due to the efforts and lucid writings of Mr. Alexander Wanless. There has at times been a certain amount of argument "about it and about", as is to be expected in the essentially conservative world of fishing, but despite everything, I am convinced that we owe a great debt of gratitude to Mr. Wanless, who, for some years, has constituted himself the prophet of the thread-line.

There has grown up, of course, a certain amount of "purism" about this type of fishing, not altogether untinged with commercialism, but the wise novice will, I hope, accept this propaganda with a certain amount of caution.

For instance, I do not believe that for thread-line fishing it is necessary to buy an expensive, rather short, split-cane rod. I myself always use a rather stiff fly rod of about eight feet six inches or even, when convenient, my ordinary dry-fly rod. I am certain that the ordinary short spinning rod is too stiff and not long enough for most of the uses to which a thread-line reel can be put. Moreover, one of the most attractive features of the fix-spool reel is that one can take one's fly rod and ordinary fly tackle plus a thread-line reel, and the few gadgets and bait required, and be lightly but fully equipped for several quite different kinds of fishing.

For argument's sake, I very often begin by fishing a dry fly up some length of river, change later to a wet fly, and later still to spinning a tiny minnow, using the same rod all the time.

This can be varied in all sorts of ways. I have, on certain days, during the past year or two, started the day by hooking and landing a salmon on a small Devon, using a nine-feet split-cane rod, and a four-pound Breaking-Strain nylon line on a thread-line reel.

For an hour or two I have, thereafter, amused myself catching a few small trout with a dry fly. . . .

Later in the afternoon I have had an amusing hour or two casting lobworms upstream over a shoal of sea trout lying on a sunny shallow, sea trout that would have been quite unapproachable by any other means at all.

When the sun was off the water in the evening, I have had another session of salmon fishing, and finished up at midnight in pitch darkness, fishing three flies in the ordinary way, for sea trout.

For this very full and varied day's fishing all I required was an ordinary nine-foot split-cane dry-fly rod, reel, etc., a thread-line reel, with 4 B.S. Nylon on it, a small tin with a few little Devons, some spinning traces, a few plain hooks, and a tin of lobworms. If you add to this a net, a gaff-head, which will screw into the net handle, a few sea-trout flies and some sea-trout casts and a few leads, it will be seen that the whole outfit will not over-crowd an ordinary fishing bag.

It may be said that all this is not exactly salmon fishing, but I think that the novice who fishes a river, at times when the use of a thread-line reel is seasonable and suitable, would be well advised also to go out prepared for the catching of sea trout and brown trout.

The actual use of a thread-line reel is one of those things which is simply a matter of a little practice and patience. I have noticed that certain old fishermen, some of whom have preconceived prejudices against these "new-fangled things", are apt to try out the thread-line method, and after a period of entanglement and bad temper, give up the whole idea of thread-lining, simply because they cannot master the very simple technique at the first attempt.

There are a few points which a beginner may like to know, which may escape him in the standard works on the subject. The first thing is the line to be used. The best line for salmon thread-line fishing is a fully-dressed line of braided nylon.

For light fishing, either for salmon or sea trout, French nylon "Monofil" is the best thing. Fine "Monofil" nylon seems to me to be rather too "springy", which makes it very apt to fly off the spool in spirals, definitely "vicious spirals", which have some unexplainable ability to get *under* the spool and round the central spindle of the reel. This is a very shocking thing indeed, and disheartening. However, if a rubber band is used to confine the nylon on the reel when not in use, and if great care is taken about never letting the line have any slack when in use, all is usually well.

The next thing to watch is this: if ever the tiniest *knot* appears on the line, the caster will have endless trouble of various sorts, and will not be able to cast a good length of line in any case.

It is quite essential to see to it that there is a complete, unbroken and unknotted length of at least forty yards on the spool, before the join between the "backing" and the line itself is reached. This is very important, in all types of line—whether braided nylon, nylon "Monofil" or dressed silk.

This last, which was what we all used before the mysterious nylon was invented, is excellent on nearly all occasions, but it is not possible to cast the lightest baits as far with dressed silk as with nylon "Monofil".

On the other hand, a silk line is much less apt to spring off the spool, or to wrap itself round the spindle under the spool.

When fishing a light Devon minnow, or a natural minnow for salmon, the great thing is to cast upstream and across, and then spin it so slowly that the minnow is almost touching the bottom. The slower a bait can be fished, for salmon, the more likelihood there is of hooking a fish. The salmon, and sometimes large sea trout, are very slow and deliberate takers.

Mr. Wanless' idea of using a float or controller for the double purpose of providing sufficient weight for casting, and for the guiding of the fly after casting is, I think, a very good idea. However, in actual practice, I have not, as yet, encountered situations where, when a fly is being used, the ordinary technique with a thirteen-feet rod is not easier and better. And yet, I can quite imagine such situations, and shall try the method whenever the opportunity presents itself.

Why so many people should have objected to this way of fishing a fly I cannot imagine. I fail to see how it matters *how* or with what you cast, so long as you get the fly over the fish in the correct manner.

One sometimes gets the impression that there are people who feel that there is some particular virtue about *casting* a fly, either for trout or salmon, with a *fly-rod*. I cannot see the point of this idea. . . .

There can be no doubt that one of the most artistic and difficult methods of salmon fishing is the technique of fishing a small shrimp, as a single hook, with a thread-line reel. This method, if a more or less freshly boiled shrimp is used, is definitely a very good way of catching salmon in places and at times when the more orthodox methods are quite futile.

Certain rivers seem to give better results in this type of fishing than others. This is so noticeable on the Conway and Lledr fishing, that many of those who kill the greater part of the fish caught each year use this thread-line shrimp technique to the exclusion of all others.

In some Irish rivers, I believe, the salmon seem to have a definite liking for prawns.

On the Lledr many of the locals dye their shrimps or small prawns by soaking them in red ink. It is interesting to speculate as to why a salmon should be attracted by a *bright red* shrimp or prawn. I have painted devon minnows bright red and fished them over the same fish that were frequently taking the red shrimps, but without the least success. There must be something attractive about a combination of the colour red and the shape and scent of a shrimp or prawn. I think that, of the three, the scent is probably the most important.

I have found a fixed-spool reel the ideal weapon for worm fishing for salmon. It always surprises me that there is a general prejudice against worm fishing for salmon, more so, I think, than against the use of a shrimp or prawn. Why this should be I cannot imagine.

For my own part, I very much prefer the honest lob-worm to the unpleasant, smelly and generally un-natural-looking prawn. The great flushed monsters which are sold by tackle dealers revoltingly preserved in glycerine are, I think, definitely offensive.

In any case, a great deal of amusement can be had by casting a lobworm upstream and across, on fast open "runs" when one knows the fish are there. On the Lledr of North Wales one can sometimes, particularly when the river is in three-quarter spate, hook one fish after another by this method. All one requires is a plain hook, a large lobworm and a medium-sized lead placed about four feet from the bait.

Cast well upstream, and across, and let everything take its course until the bait begins to bend your rod as it hangs downstream; then wind in *very slowly*.

You will need plenty of hooks and plenty of nylon, and any amount of big lobworms for this exercise, as you will be constantly hung up behind by stones and small rocks.

In this sort of fishing it is frequently quite impossible

to tell the difference between the taking of a fish and one of the frequent "hang-ups". When you see that the bait has checked, and that it has either been taken by a salmon or has fouled a rock, strike firmly but not jerkily; it is astonishing how often it *is* a salmon and not a rock.

In summer fishing the only really distressing thing about this fishing is that you so often hook eels when "rolling" your worm down in the manner described. There have been times when the eels have more or less spoilt my fishing; others when the eels seem to leave one's bait severely alone.

In more orthodox salmon fishing when a salmon has been firmly struck and hooked, especially when one is using a large spring bait in spring fishing, the number of fish lost is quite small.

In thread-line fishing for salmon, notably in fast rocky rivers, one's troubles are only just beginning when a fish has been hooked. When a four-pound breaking-strain line is used, the margin of error permissible is not very great, and for quite a while one has comparatively little control of one's fish.

Undoubtedly a good deal of skill is required to land any large proportion of the salmon hooked. For this reason I think this thread-line technique infinitely the most sporting way of fishing for salmon.

Here again is "one of those things" which nothing except actual experience will avail the novice. No amount of written instruction will help very much when the beginner suddenly finds himself "fast" into a lively fish in heavy water, with perhaps a quite impossible stretch of white water and boulders fifty yards below him.

Mr. Wanless' instructions about slacking off when your hooked fish threatens to "go out of the pool" is absolutely correct, of course, but I personally think it is one of the very hardest things to do. It can be done, of course, and is constantly done by experienced fishers but the beginner will appreciate exactly what I mean when the actual necessity confronts him.

However, on ordinary occasions the running of a fish with a thread-line reel is a quite simple matter.

I would advise the novice *not* to rely too much on his "slipping clutch", as in practice I have found that the tension has a habit—at the critical moment—of being either too tight or too slack. I think, on the whole, that the best and safest thing is to set the tension so that the clutch will only slip when the maximum amount of strain is being put upon the line.

When a fish is hooked, just use the reel like any other reel—but be very careful that the revolving handle does not catch on your sleeve or coat or in your gaff-strap, for that will mean "the end". However, it is quite astonishing what strain can be put on to a very thin-looking four- or five-pound line, if you are using, say, a nine-feet rod, with a "dry-fly action".

The beginner can test the truth of this very simply (probably involuntarily) by noticing the vast amount of strength needed to break the line, when he has become immovably and irredeemably fastened to a tree root or behind some boulder.

In any case, he who fishes for and hooks salmon by the thread-line method will have all the fun of the fair, and feel suitably proud of himself when he has landed a good fish by this method.

CHAPTER XI

SOME SUGGESTIONS ABOUT WHERE TO FISH

THERE can be no doubt that the belief is very general that salmon fishing is essentially for the rich, and that the poor man had better content himself with trout or coarse fishing.

It is rather natural that this should be so, for undoubtedly the very best of salmon fishing is extremely expensive. So, for that matter, is the best of every type of sport. The best dry-fly trout fishing is even more expensive and hard to come by than salmon fishing; some very special loch fishing is amazingly expensive. I know of a house and three small lochs which the owner used to let before the war, quite easily, for £300 per month in June and July. However, the "House" was a place to dream about, and the fishing as nearly perfect as anything could be; the trout averaged over three pounds!

And yet, when one really looks into the matter, it will be found that salmon fishing—good, but not supremely good fishing—can be enjoyed all over the British Isles at a quite reasonable cost. It is not the *fishing* which will cost you money nowadays, but your living expenses.

For the benefit of anyone who has not fished very much for salmon, I think a few suggestions about where to fish and where to stay might be of interest.

There is one thing, however, about all salmon fishing which should never be overlooked: the uncertainty. You may start a considerable overdraft at the bank, or part with the savings of years to lease two or three miles of the Dee, and catch five kelts and no salmon in the month of March, or you may stay for the night, more or less by chance, at the inn in a village you had never heard of before, and land four salmon the next day on a five-shilling ticket. . . . Roughly speaking, I have done both these things myself.

No, salmon fishing is always something of a gamble; perhaps that is why so many rich and successful gamblers like it . . . I wouldn't know.

Starting with the West Country, there is plenty of good, and as I think, cheap salmon fishing at a number of places. The Taw, for instance, can be fished at South Molton Road in Devonshire, from the Fortescue Arms in the early part of the year, and the Tavy, Walkam and Plym Fishing Association of Tavistock has any amount of good fishing which is well worth the trying.

There is fishing to be had in many different rivers and places in Devon, and the best way to fish it is to wander about in a car, and make inquiries. . . . Watch-makers and jewellers, hotel proprietors and tackle-makers usually know between them all that is possible to know about any local fishing.

You may ask: "Why watch-makers and jewellers?" and I cannot tell you. You will find, however, that up and down England and Scotland it is very frequently the owner of some small jewellers shop who knows more about the local fishing than anyone else.

Moving rather further north, there is always a chance of a few salmon from the great and solemn Wye, if inquiries are made at the Beaufort Hotel at

Tintern, or a variety of places in the Holme Lacy neighbourhood. The best beats on the Wye are, of course, very much taken up, but like the Tweed, it is often possible to get an occasional week or a few days by making inquiries on the spot.

Another good river, is the Usk. The hotel at Crickhowell knows all about it, and can often get a visitor some really good fishing. There is also water to be fished through the hotels in Usk, Abergavenny and Brecon, also at the Glangrwyney Hotel near Crickhowell. This Usk fishing used to be very good indeed, but is not as good as before the War.

The salmon fishing in the Dovey, much further north in Wales, is not too good, but a stay at Machynlleth is well worth while, if only to gain information about the very first-class sea-trout fishing in this delightful river.

The Teifi in Cardiganshire is undoubtedly one of the most beautiful-*looking* salmon rivers in any country, but this river is fished and poached in the most astonishing way by the local coracle men. I was once discussing this matter with a cheerful fisher of those parts, who quite openly knew a great deal about this coracle poaching.

His attitude is summed up by his remark that the coracle men had been fishing as they liked since before Julius Caesar landed, and did not see why they should not continue. This, of course, is all very well, but the fact remains that one of the finest salmon rivers in the country has been almost ruined as a result.

Anyone who would like to explore this lovely river, would be well advised to call on Mr. Tommy Davies, Saddler, of Newcastle Emlyn, who is a very fine fisherman himself, and is also a veritable mine of information.

Now we come to what I think is quite the best salmon fishing open to more or less casual visitors in either England or Wales. Curiously enough the Conway and Lledr fishings are not really well-known to most salmon fishers, but there is a select band of very talented fishers who catch a vast number of salmon each season on these two beautiful rivers.

The headquarters of this fishing is the Gwydyr Hotel at Bettws-y-Coed, where Mrs. Cornell Smith, the proprietress, controls a very excellently run association, which owns or leases much of the best fishing in the district.

Actual membership of this association is very difficult to obtain nowadays, but permits of various categories are issued for daily, weekly or monthly periods for various parts of the Conway.

For approximately fifteen shillings per day a visitor can fish several miles of really first-class water, on which there are seven or eight casts which are all that any salmon fisher could want. On this ticket water of the association on the Conway, all baits arc permitted on most of the pools, and this is the "capital", as it were, of the thread-line shrimp technique.

The one thing which any visitor should definitely *not* forget is a large bottle of freshly boiled shrimps. He will find that most of the local fishermen use nothing else.

Actually, a great number of fish are caught each season on the fly, and very many on either Devon minnows or golden sprats. In fact, this is really good all-round fishing.

From July onwards it is as good sea-trout fishing as will be found anywhere.

During the 1948 season over five hundred salmon

were landed on the Lledr and Conway. Late in the season a great many fish are caught up the Lledr at Pont-y-Pant and Dolwyddelan on the local association water, who issue very cheap day tickets.

You will *see* more salmon up the Lledr in a day than most people see in half a life-time, but the dourness of these fish that have braved the roaring gorge between the Conway Junction and Pont-y-Pant is quite remarkable.

The Welsh Dee is, of course, one of the really great salmon rivers, but as far as I know the really good beats are not to be fished by outsiders, except on very rare occasions.

However, some quite good fishing can be had from the Dee Fishery Board at Chester. Sometimes it is possible to get a week or two's fishing in the very excellent Overton district by application to the Byny-Pys Estate Office at Overton.

The very comfortable Hand Hotel at Llangollen has at least one good pool for their guests, and will give much information about other club fishings between Llangollen and Corwen.

This is a lovely bit of river, which is worth fishing even on the blankest of blank days.

Still going north, I think the next place where a salmon can be killed is probably at some point on the Lune in North-West Lancashire. I know little about this river, except that it looks good, and can be fished at various places by ticket.

I once met a man who went for a picnic with his family in May or early June to some place near Caton, close to Lancaster. To amuse himself he bought a five-shilling ticket from an hotel, and proceeded to fish for trout in rather a desultory way.

He saw a salmon rise in the neck of a nice pool, and

putting on a sea-trout fly, had a cast or two over him. He rose, was hooked and duly landed, and weighed ten pounds.

Within half an hour the picnicker had another of thirteen pounds, and later lost another fish. . . . All this on a five-shilling ticket, weeks after the presumed end of the spring fishing, which illustrates the uncertainty I mentioned earlier.

After the Lune, I would advise my novice friend to make straight for the excellent tackle shop of Mr. Strong in Carlisle. For fishing throughout the whole of the Western Border, there is nobody who can and will give such good advice about fishing on the Eden, Border Esk, Annan, etc.

There are any amount of salmon rivers and salmon fishings in the neighbourhood of Carlisle, Longtown and Langholm, but for some reason the salmon fishing of the Border Esk, which should be excellent, is nearly always disappointing. Sea-trout fishing, on which, by the way, Mr. Strong is a real expert, is quite another matter. It is definitely first class.

One of the pleasantest and most pleasantly managed fishing hotels in the country is the Cross Keys at Cannonbie on the Esk, where Mr. Miller is a great and keen fisherman, and a delightful companion.

Incidentally, I have forgotten to mention that there is some excellent fishing to be had by ticket in West Cumberland, at Cockermouth. I believe, although I have never fished there myself, that the Derwent here is really good. The Castle Fishery of Cockermouth, would give all information and advise.

On the other side of England, rather more to the south, is the Yorkshire Esk—a river which has been more or less rejuvenated within the past twenty or thirty years. I believe it can be quite good. Most of the fishing is controlled by the Esk Fishing Board of Whitby, who issue permits.

In Northumberland are, of course, the Coquet and Tyne, but these rivers are more or less unknown to me personally. Messrs. Hardy Bros. of Alnwick would, of course, give all information.

The astonishing thing is that salmon are still killed on the Tyne.... How any fish manages to get through the black horror of the river at Newcastle is beyond my comprehension.

The fishing round Hexham used to be very good, but I do not think it is worth fishing as far as salmon are concerned nowadays. The Coquet is a good sea-trout river, but the salmon fishing, except in one or two privately owned pools is not too good, I hear.

We come now to a great river, a noble river, and, I think, the best fishing district in Britain—the Tweed. The difficulties and expense of getting on to such famous fishings as North Wark, Sprouston, Carham, Floors or Hendersyde are obvious, but I would strongly advise the keen novice salmon fisher to go to Mr. Forrest's tackle shop in Kelso at the first opportunity. Here he will hear all about the possibilities and impossibilities of the various fishings but, if he is lucky, he may find that an odd few days, a week or even a fortnight, is to be let to a suitable tenant on one of the good beats. This does not happen very often, but it does happen *sometimes*.

A friend of mine once took a chance ten days on Carham and killed over forty salmon.

As I mentioned in my earlier remarks about trout fishing, I would make Tillmouth Castle Hotel, or the Collingwood Arms my headquarters when on Tweed in the spring. At the Tillmouth a real fisherman, even a beginner, will be able to find out many things about

RIVER SHIEL, NEAR KENTRA, ACHARACLE

Judges Ltd.

"TYN-Y-CAI." THE JUNCTION POOL OF THE CONWAY AND LLEDR RIVERS, NORTH WALES

the various fishings which he would not be likely to discover in any other way. In any case, he will be able to fish parts of the lower Till and, I would advise him to try for the remarkable sea trout—all very big fish, that run in Tweed and up Till in the winter, and that return to the estuary in March and April.

Some very interesting things have been discovered in recent years by Mr. G. H. Nall about these big sea trout, and certain thread-line fishers have had extraordinary sport during the past few springs.

The whole atmosphere of Tweedside seems, somehow, connected with the river and fishing. In its lovely and fertile valley the Tweed seems like the Nile, to influence the lives of all who live there. If any young or inexperienced fisherman should chance to live on Tweedside for a time, and is, at heart, a real fisher, it will not be long before he ceases to be inexperienced or a novice. Tweedside is the greatest of all angling instructors. . . .

Travelling north from the Border I think the next place to make for is Perth, and the kingdom of Messrs. Malloch, who can advise the inquirer about any sort of fishing from a five-shilling day ticket on some local club water, to the lease of the most famous salmon casts in Britain.

It is no exaggeration to say that the firm of Malloch is or has been in touch with everything connected with fishing in Scotland.

I personally know little or nothing about the Tay fishing, or the relative merits of the many rivers of the Tay watershed, but I do know that Mallochs know.

In Glen Lyon there is the Fortingal Hotel, which I know is, or was, until recently, able to find some really excellent fishing for its guests. The Tummel, of course, can be first class, and if the visitor is of an

G

insensitive and phlegmatic temperament, he may, at
a moderate expense, catch a large salmon in Loch
Tay so early in the year, and in such arctic weather
that it makes me shudder even to write about it.

I believe that Killin is the starting point for these
polar expeditions. Hereabouts, there obtains the
somewhat foreign custom of charging something over
£1 for each salmon caught.

Travelling north again, some very excellent fishing
can be enjoyed in either of those charming rivers of
Scotland's east coast, the North and South Esk. The
Panmure Arms at Edzell knows all about the fishing,
and I believe the Dalhousie Estate grants fishing permits.

And very soon now we must come to the Dee, and
salmon casts as productive, famous and as expensive as
Tweed's Sprouston, Wark or Carham.

From the tidal water near Aberdeen, right up to
Braemar, there is one celebrated fishery after another.
The number of spring fish caught within six or seven
miles of Banchory must be very great, but the Dee is
not, I think, the best of rivers from a casual visitor's
point of view.

I do not think that as many good casts have been
acquired by associations or hotels as on the Tweed, for
instance. I have no doubt that odd days and weeks
can be booked, but my advice to the beginner is to
consult Messrs. Playfair in Aberdeen, the fishing-tackle
manufacturers, and the makers of the unsurpassed
"Vibration" rods, which I have mentioned previously.
If any fishing is procurable, they will know about it,
and give the best of advice about methods of fishing,
either with fly or bait.

Going still north, the Don at Alford Bridge, very
famous for its excellent trout fishing, can be very good

for salmon, if one is lucky and well-instructed. The
Forbes Arms at Alford Bridge can usually arrange some
fishing, and is in any case a very comfortable hotel.

At Huntly, also a good centre for trout fishing, later
in the year, the novice will find that he can get any
amount of salmon fishing at a comparatively reasonable cost on the Town Water of the Deveron, which,
when the water is right, provides salmon fishing on a
few really nice casts. There are a number of private
lengths of the Deveron, such as Rothiemay, which are
first-class, but these beats are nearly always fully let,
and for one reason or another, occasional days or
weeks are not easily arranged.

When on the Deveron, the keen fisherman should
certainly make careful inquiries about certain fishings
which are not at all well-known. One of them, which
I will not specify by name, is dependent upon the
amount of water in April and May.

My imaginary "beginner" should by the time he
has reached the Deveron, be cunning in the ways of
finding out all about little-known fishings. . . . He will
have been well educated by my friends the jewellers
and watch-makers, so with this hint about "water in
April and May", he should be able to find a certain
quiet pool where he may receive quite a shock and
maybe catch a salmon or two, all for the present price
of a packet of cigarettes.

After reaching the Deveron, the number of places
where one can fish for and *perhaps* catch salmon,
become so numerous that it would be a long, long
business to catalogue them all. Rivers like the Spey,
Thurso, Findhorn, the Naver and Helmsdale, to
mention only a few, can all be fished by various means,
expensively or cheaply, but I would advise my much-
travelled novice not to scorn certain loch fishings

where, although the main concentration may be on
sea trout, it is frequently possible to have really good
sport with salmon.

Anyone who can manage to wander about the
North-West and West of Scotland looking for salmon
fishing may well be astonished at the amount of really
pleasant fishing to be enjoyed in all sorts of unexpected
places.

Lastly, I would draw the attention of every true
fisher to that almost forgotten country of South-West
Scotland, Galloway. The little rivers of Fleet, Luce
and Cree and the larger river of the Kirkcudbright-
shire Dee, are all at certain heights of water really
good salmon rivers—the Cree can be very good indeed.

Gatehouse of Fleet, Newton Stewart and Kirkcudbright are the obvious centres for exploring and fishing
this lovely corner of Scotland.

The wild, almost roadless country in behind Cairnsmore of Fleet and Merrick, and around that remote
and white-lipped loch, Enoch, is known to very few
people, even in these days.

Those who know it best, apart from the Galloway
shepherds, must be those fated and dedicated young
men of our Commandos, who spent such arduous and
comfortless days and nights in these lonely hills, during
their war-time training.

Here then, are just a few suggestions for the novice
salmon fisher, which I hope may be of use to him.

PART III

ON THE CATCHING OF SEA TROUT

CHAPTER XII

DAY-TIME FISHING FOR SEA TROUT

I THINK that the only word that really describes the sea trout is "incomprehensible". . . .

The trout of the common or stay-at-home variety is a simple and guileless creature compared to his sea-faring relative. The salmon, the large and crazy cousin of the sea trout, is also incomprehensible, but nothing like so eccentric.

All my life, since the day when as a small boy I caught one tiny and argent finnoch in the salt water of Loch Sunart when mackerel fishing, I have followed the gleaming sea trout as men once sought the Holy Grail.

I have had days that were very nearly good days, and nights that just missed being unforgettable. I have walked hundreds of miles, risked life and limb and pneumonia countless times; in Shetland I have walked for miles into winds that you could lean on, as if against a wall, over deserts of small boulders, with the gulls mocking me, to find that in the sandy voe of my choice there were no sea trout shoals, but two large and smiling seals.

85

I have been lost in a steamy and midge-haunted birch wood of the West Coast, in the small hours of the morning, with a broken electric torch and a very nearly broken heart, after losing a dozen large sea trout.

I have slipped and fallen off slippery rocks into cold and deep rivers in Argyll; in North Wales, in South Wales and into the sea in Unst in Shetland.

And after all my adventures and agonies, the number of warrantable sea trout I have caught must be comparatively small. And that is why, I think, I love sea-trout fishing above all other forms of the Delightful Delusion.

To him who has never fished for sea trout, but who is still an honest man and a true fisher, I should like to offer a few hints and suggestions, for what they are worth. For some reason, many others who have written about sea-trout fishing seem to have caught sea trout in vast numbers and with, to me, really infuriating ease. Why should I, who love a four-pound sea trout much more than I do most of my fellow-men, have been so sorely tried in my fishing?

However, my very failures and sorrows may have fitted me to some slight degree for the instruction and warning of others.

To begin with then, we will dwell upon the catching of sea trout and finnoch in the day-time . . . later we will come to the mystic delights of night fishing.

*   *   *   *   *

I think that the most important thing to remember about day-light sea-trout fishing is vibration. I am convinced that the hearing or sound sense of the sea trout is even more sensitive than that of the brown trout. The salmon seems definitely less affected by

either sound or sight than his smaller relatives . . .
or is it just contempt for *homo sapiens*?

I suppose that the best type of water for the catching
of sea trout in day-time is some shallow but fast and
broken water on a big river. On the Border Esk, for
instance, sea trout will frequently take quite well if one
wades *up* a ford where one knows that the shoals are
lying, and fishes an ordinary cast of three flies over
them.

Herling do definitely take well when this method is
used; big sea trout much more infrequently.

It is very important to find out exactly when the
first shoals of big sea trout arrive in the river, as the
best, perhaps the only really good time for getting them
in the day-time, is during the first few days after their
arrival.

On the Esk, for example, this may happen any time
after the 1st of June, usually about the 7th or 8th of the
month, given suitable water.

In the Shiel River of Moidart the big sea trout arrive
every year almost monotonously on the 1st of June,
but here this regularity is helped by the fact that the
height of the water usually has little or no influence
on the run of fish, who are able to swim into the sea
pool on every high tide.

On the Teifi, in South Wales, I have never heard of
any really good sport being enjoyed with sea trout in the
day-time—the Dovey is better in this respect, I believe.

The Conway, again, is almost hopeless before night-
fall unless one uses the thread-line minnow technique.
Without any doubt the nearer you are to the tide, the
better chance you have in day-time fishing. Night
fishing, curiously enough, is not so good in sea pools or
salt water.

In the Hebrides, Shetland and Orkney, the sea

trout seem to take very well during the day, and do not seem to be so affected by vibration. I have always found that in windy, wild places, within sound of the sea, the sea trout's sensitiveness seems blunted. I suppose the constant slight vibration caused by the waves and the movement of the sea is the cause of this.

I have constantly read and heard about sea trout being caught on a dry-fly. This always puzzles me, as I have tried all my small stock of cunning in this way for years in all sorts of places with the most meagre results. And yet hundreds of good sea trout are caught each year on a dry-fly. Since writing this I have heard of big sea trout being caught frequently on the lower reaches of the Otter in Devon. Evidently I just do not know how to do it!

I once, when very young, thought I had found the ideal way of sea-trout fishing. I was sitting on a lonely little rock point of the Shiel River known as Grassy Point, waiting for the sun to get off the water, before I started to put a fly over a salmon that kept "head and tailing" just below the point. While I sat there I kept seeing good sea trout rise, just like brown trout, in the glassy run off the rock in front of me.

As the sun showed no signs of disappearing, I went up to the farm and fetched my nine-foot rod, a 5X cast and some dry flies.

Without much thought of anything happening, I floated a large, dark Varient over these rising sea trout. The very first time over, a big sea trout rose and took the fly, for all the world like a three-pounder on the Test or Kennet.

I landed this nice trout of two and a half pounds after quite an exciting five minutes of acrobatics, and prepared to get another one.

I fished for an hour or more, thereafter, over many

rising sea trout, but never in that time did even one trout take any apparent interest in any floating fly I could show him.

I often tried this dry-fly idea afterwards on the Shiel and elsewhere, but never rose another fish until years afterwards on the Conway in Wales, when I did rise and land a small three-quarter-pound sea trout on a floating Tup.

I would therefore advise the beginner (or anyone else) not to bother about the dry-fly method over sea trout, unless, like I do, he prefers to try everything at least once.

Sometimes on a hot day, when you see shoals of sea trout lying upstream of you in an easily reached shallow, it seems almost inconceivable that they will not take either a floating fly or a nymph—but in my experience they very rarely do. I have a much better drill for this sort of occasion, which I will mention in a later chapter.

I believe that in the West Irish loughs and tidal streams, the sea trout, which, by the way, average a good deal less in weight than the Scottish or Welsh trout, do indeed take really well in the day-time. In Lewis and other Hebridean islands this also applies. Loch Boisdale's remarkably varied fishings are all day-time casts. The same applies in certain sea pools and sea lochs of the mainland.

In Shetland, one rarely fishes at night, except perhaps in July, and as night is much the same as day as far as light is concerned, the state of the tide, and the absence or presence of seals, has much more influence on one's success or failure than the actual time of day.

In the Shetland voe-fishing, where one is actually fishing in the sea itself, the trout do indeed "take a fly", if indeed the "cardinal lures" and other con-

traptions such as strips of mackerel skin that one uses
can be called "flies". . . .

This is very amusing fishing, but I would urge anyone who does not know Shetland to make a point of
studying the prevailing wind very carefully before
actually setting out on what may well be an extremely
arduous day's walking. If one is careful about this, it
is nearly always possible to fix upon a few voes which
are sheltered from the wind. . . . It must be understood
that there is nearly always a nice fresh breeze, which
in other places would be called a gale, and if this
boreal breeze is hitting a voe or bay, it is quite impossible to fish there. The sea trout also seem to like the
more sheltered voes—so, unfortunately, do the seals.
So there you have the main factors in Shetland fishing
—Wind, Tide and Seals.

If, as happens about half a dozen times in a season,
one finds a nicely sheltered voe, with the sun shining
and the sea-trout shoals cruising above the sandy
bottom in full view (sea trout look *brown*, by the way,
in the sea) *and* there is no seal or seals present, it is
possible to have an hour or two's fishing which will be
really memorable. A two- or three-pound sea trout,
hooked in the salt-water, does indeed fight in the most
astonishing way. For this sort of fishing it is better to
use pretty strong gut, or nylon, as you will frequently
be fishing near or in the seaweed, and very light gut
would never stand the strain of being wrapped round
clumps of weed with a sea trout at one end and you at
the other.

The brown-trout fishing is quite good in a few lochs
in Shetland, and very often the sea trout will be there
as well. On the whole, however, I do not think a
so-called fly is the best thing to fish with in Shetland,
as I will explain later.

CHAPTER XIII

THREAD-LINE FISHING WITH A MINNOW OR LOBWORM, FOR SEA TROUT IN SHETLAND AND ELSEWHERE

As one who could not care less what the purists or the fly-only men think, I would urge every boy, young man or novice angler to see to it that he becomes and remains a "free fisher".... By a "free fisher" I mean one who fishes in exactly the way he thinks fit, and sporting. The basis of happiness in fishing, as in most other phases of existence, is freedom. This does not mean that one should be a poacher; on the contrary, a really "free fisher" will respect the freedom of other fishers and their privacy.

The man who secretly and feloniously lures a great trout at Leckford or Ramsbury with an irresistible lobworm, commits a monstrous crime against the brotherhood of honest men and fishermen, and against a noble trout.

On the other hand, the man who insists upon using "a fly only" in Shetland, even if "the fly" used is a two-inch Cardinal Lure, and at the same time sneers at the skilled caster of a lobworm, is a nuisance and as I think, rather silly.

By all means use a fly, if that form of fishing for sea trout appeals to you, but for heaven's sake, do not cherish the thought that this is the only or even the best way of sea-trout fishing.

In recent years, fishing West-Highland rivers, and
rivers in North Wales, I have amused myself by evol-
ving, at any rate to my own great satisfaction, a
thread-line technique for sea-trout fishing which I
personally find much more interesting than the time-
honoured method of downstream wet-fly fishing;
night and evening fishing excepted.

In the first place, let us consider the use of a small
natural or devon minnow in the day-time.

This day-time spinning for sea trout seems to be
very little use except on big, wide rivers, or on certain
lochs.

I first realized the possibilities of this light, long-
range spinning for sea trout a few years ago on the
Conway.

Very few sea trout are caught on the fly in this good
river, in the day-time; at night the local fishermen and
others enjoy as good sea-trout fishing as can be found
anywhere. A few people have always caught *a few*
good sea trout during the day with a minnow, but I
was surprised in the summer of 1946 at a time when
very few sea trout were being caught, even by the
local night fishers, to find that my son, who seems to
have developed his own particular technique of
thread-line spinning, began to bring in anything up to
half a dozen good sea trout almost every day.

As far as I can understand his method of procedure,
there are a few definite rules which do appear to have
a great influence on the success of the whole exercise. . . .

Firstly, it is necessary to make very long casts—as
long as possible—with a very light bait. This can only
be done in my experience by using "Monifil" nylon
lines of less than four pounds breaking strain, and when
the spool of the reel has been filled right up to the lip.

It is also quite essential to be sure that there is at least forty or fifty yards of line entirely free from any joint or knot. This is necessary because with a comparatively "whippy" rod and with the wind behind you, casts of forty or even fifty yards are quite possible.

Secondly, a bait, either natural or artificial, should not be more than one inch in length, and as light as possible, taking into account the length of cast required; half-inch Devons are even better if procurable.

My son always used very small gold and brown Devon minnows, with, of course, one small treble in the tail. I myself have often used a very small natural minnow on an "Aerial" flight, but have never had quite the same success, as far as sea trout are concerned, as with the small Devon. Brown trout, on the other hand, definitely prefer the natural bait.

Thirdly, the cast must be made squarely across the stream, slightly upstream if possible. When the bait hits the water, if there is a good level run that is not less than four feet deep, do not begin to wind at once, but let the bait sink and move down the current.

When you reckon the minnow is level with you, or slightly downstream, begin to wind in *very slowly*. I must confess that I have never quite discovered the actual action of the bait while this is happening, but the sea trout seem to take it on an almost slack line, so that it cannot be really spinning in the ordinary way.

Of course, this technique is only really possible in a large river, with a rather heavy flow and in a place which is more or less clear of big rocks.

The ideal place is one where you can wade out on shingle and cast right under the far bank into a deep, fast stream. The best height of water for all this is, as in spinning generally, when the river is clearing after a spate, and is "big" but only slightly coloured.

Incidentally, this method of spinning seems very
good for salmon as well as sea trout, on certain
occasions. I think this is a most admirable and
sporting way of catching sea trout, and should appeal
to those who do not like night fishing. This technique,
and another which I will mention later, does enable
one to enjoy whole days of sea-trout fishing in places
and at times when to "flog" down the river with "a
cast of flies" would be quite futile.

*   *   *   *   *

Another very productive and amusing method of
catching sea trout is, happily enough, best practiced
when there is a blazing sun above a dead low river in
late July or August. I refer to the artistic and delicate
technique of casting our old and faithful friend—the
lobworm.

Unlike the thread-line minnow technique, which I
have just described, this worm fishing, with very fine
casting tackle, is for the fishing of small west-coast
rivers and sea pools.

It will be remembered that the summer of 1947 was
most unusually hot and sunny, especially on the west
coast of Scotland. All sea-trout fishing in the ordinary
way was almost hopelessly bad. On some of the smaller
rivers the sea trout simply would not, in many cases,
could not, run up far beyond the sea pools. In our little
river the shoals of sea trout and finnoch made a
practice of coming in on the high tide and I used to
watch them questing upstream in a nervous and tenta-
tive sort of way. I never saw them go beyond a pool
about half a mile above the tide, and even in that pool
they fussed about uneasily for a time, and then made
off down again to the sea pool.

Night fishing was quite useless as the pools well up the river held no sea trout and, as is usually the case, they did not take a fly well at night in the sea pool itself.

On this little river I have mentioned, we used to watch big shoals of small sea trout and finnoch lying in rows in about eighteen inches of water right down on the shingle of the sea-pool's tail. One hot day I thought I would try an experiment.

I fixed up my ordinary light spinning outfit, but instead of a minnow I put on one large lobworm, but no lead or weight.

I got right down below the shingle bar at the tail of the sea pool, and crawled slowly and quietly up the thin rippling water until I was about twenty yards immediately below the shoals.

Keeping down very low, I cast the lobworm upstream so that it landed with a considerable commotion right among the basking sea trout. What happened then was, I think, very instructive. The trout, of course, scattered all over the tail of the pool when the lobworm landed among them. I left everything alone and allowed the worm to sink and lie on the shingle.

The sea trout circled round for a moment or two, and then several of them returned, evidently to find out what it was that had caused this disturbance.

They then found nothing more alarming than a very large worm crawling about among the stones. The worm was then taken without any hesitation, but, curiously enough, not retained.

The first trout that obliged in this way seized the worm, held it for a second or two and then dropped it. He then swam round in a small circle and returned again to the worm and took it properly.

Within twenty minutes I had out three sea trout and missed one or two more.

In this sort of fishing, like dry-fly fishing, one has the advantage of being able to pull a hooked fish downstream and to play him there without alarming the other fish in the pool above. A few days later, one or two of us began to fish another river—a river larger than our own, but with the most notable reputation of "dourness".

In this river we found immense shoals of sea trout and finnoch, lying all over the shallow pools not far above the high-tide mark.

Using this upstream technique, we had nearly seventy sea trout and finnoch in three rather desultory afternoon's fishing.

I have since used this method on various rivers with very marked success. Apart from the fact that one can catch sea trout when conditions would normally be considered to be quite hopeless, it is always exciting to be able to see your sea trout and to cast over them much as one would approach and try for a big trout in a chalk stream.

In this sort of fishing, I think that it is absolutely essential to use a very fine line, say a two-pound Breaking-Strain nylon, *and* a trace of 4X gut made up with one very tiny swivel. A three-pound sea trout, fresh from the sea loch, on such tackle, has to be treated with some respect.

I think that this variant of the "upstream worm" method can be developed and is, I am sure, a most artistic and sporting method of catching sea trout in low water.

*   *   *   *   *

At one time I used to go to Shetland with two good

John Rae

LOCH ETIVE, ARGYLL, LOOKING TO THE HILLS OF GLENCOE. IMMENSE NUMBERS OF SEA-TROUT
ENTER LOCH ETIVE TO ASCEND LATER THE MANY STREAMS WHICH ENTER THE LOCH

A BURN RUNNING DOWN INTO THE HEAD OF A VOE, SHETLAND

old friends of mine, who had family connections in those parts. These good and keen fishers were notable sufferers from the "fly only" complex even when they were fishing in the sea voes.

I was amused to find that when, as often happened, we heard about some local fisherman having had a dozen or so good sea trout the day before, my friends always ended any comment on the happening by saying "Of course, on a worm. . . ."

Why the taking of sea trout on a worm should be in any less worthy than the much more infrequent hooking of them on a huge and hideous "lure" seemed, and still seems to me, quite illogical.

Despite a certain well-defined air of disapproval, I soon began to catch really good sea trout, fishing from a small "pram" among the thick weed at the head of the nearest voe, casting a worm over any good fish I saw jump. I had some really good fun this way, but it was not until considerably later that the idea of casting a lobworm with a fixed-spool reel occurred to me.

To anyone who thinks of trying the Orkney or Shetland fishing, I would heartily recommend this technique. In these Northern Islands, after July, the shoals of sea trout cruise about in the voes frequently right among the weed clumps, waiting for the autumn rains to make the burns navigable.

Almost at any time, good sea trout can be seen jumping in the shallow water at the heads of the voes, but it is a fruitless business trying to fish a fly or lure over them on account of the weed.

Any form of spinning is quite hopeless, too. What fly fishing is possible must, therefore, be practiced in the sandy bays where there is little or no weed, but where there are also fewer sea trout.

The drill for this worm-casting technique is roughly

H

as follows: use an ordinary stiff-actioned fly rod and
any sort of efficient thread-line reel, a four-pound
Breaking-Strain nylon line, and a rather large plain
hook. No swivel is necessary, and you can put the
hook straight on to the line.

In some voes it may be possible to wade out sufficiently far to reach any jumping trout, but if it can be
managed, a light boat, sculled by paddle from the
stern, is much the best thing.

Although I have not had an opportunity of trying
it, I think a rubber dinghy would be excellent for this
purpose, as one could move about from voe to voe
and always have a boat on hand. How a rubber
dinghy would like a "breeze", in Shetland, I do not
know!

Move out very quietly through the weed, watching
all the time for a trout to move or jump. When you do
see a fish move, try to drop a lobworm as nearly into
the rings made by the trout's jump as possible. The
quicker you are about doing this the better, as sea-
trout shoals are usually moving about very quickly.

When the worm lands in the water, do not wind in
or jerk it in any way; simply let the worm sink. Very
frequently it does not actually sink, but as the line is
probably over a weed clump, remains suspended a
foot or two under the water.

Do nothing at all . . . just watch your line. In actual
practice, if you manage to drop the worm quickly
enough over the place where the trout has jumped,
you will not have to wait more than a second or two
before you see the line "shoot" and you are into a fish.
Curiously enough, you need not worry much about
getting "weeded" in the chalk-stream sense. For some
reason, given reasonably strong nylon, it is not often
that seaweed interferes much with the playing of a sea

trout. I don't know why this should be so, but I am content to think it is "just one of those things".

Only last year I had a four-and-a-half-pound sea trout in a sea loch, on an ordinary Peter Ross fly incidentally, which took me right on the edge of a vast area of heavy seaweed. In the course of the ensuing excitement he was in and out of this weed forest continually, but I was never really hung-up for a moment.

This thread-lining for sea trout in salt water in Shetland or in any suitable sea loch in Scotland, is the very greatest fun. If you can only manage to locate a shoal of sea trout or finnoch and can get your bait over it quickly, before it moves too far away, you are almost sure to get into a fish.

I have watched and fished over any amount of trout in Shetland and elsewhere when using a fly or lure, and have observed what happens. They seem almost frightened of the fly, and keep following it and "pecking" at it, as it were. When you hook one, it is more often than not almost a fluke, and I have hardly ever seen a trout, except occasionally a really big one, take the fly in a confident and determined manner. On the other hand, a sea trout does actually take a worm with the utmost confidence, and certainty. In fact, when a trout, in the sea, takes a worm he is actually feeding whereas with a fly or lure he is merely hitting at it in a half-angry, half-frightened manner.

One of the most noticeable things about catching sea trout with very fine tackle in a voe or a sea loch, is the almost frantic fight they put up when hooked. Even a three- or four-pound fish will fly about and jump like a half-pound finnoch. It is altogether a most amusing way of fishing, and well worth anyone's while trying.

Incidentally, oil your reel, *all over*, every night after fishing in salt water, and at the same time give your rod a rub down with an oil rag, particularly the rings, and reel-fittings. The effect of salt-water on a thread-line reel can be quite devastating.

CHAPTER XIV

EVENING AND NIGHT FISHING FOR SEA TROUT WITH A FLY

EVENING and night fishing for sea trout is one of those things that one either loves or hates. . . . I have met very many fishermen who dislike it violently, and for that reason rarely, if ever, get any sea-trout fishing at all. Others, myself among them, consider that the fleeting brief periods when the big sea trout are really on the move and the midge attacks have reached a crescendo of fury, are the most precious of all fishing times. . . .

I think there is some understandable confusion of thought about this matter.

Night fishing for sea trout can be two or more very different things, dependent upon when you fish and where.

To fish during the later half of June or in July on a West-Highland river from 10.30 p.m. to 12 o'clock or later is really only twilight fishing, or fishing when the sun is finally "off the water". There is still plenty of light for ordinary purposes and there is a quiet magic and beauty about the whole thing which is what most of us mean when we speak of night fishing.

The other kind of night fishing—the sort of fishing which so many people dislike—is quite another matter. Night fishing in England or Wales can be a very dour business indeed. To flog away into the inky blackness

of some tree-shadowed pool; to be unable to see even
the point of one's rod, let alone the flies or cast; to be
unable to see a rise or to tell where a hooked fish is at
any given moment is not likely to be a very popular
form of fishing.

And yet, there are dozens of people who prefer this
sort of fishing to any other. There is tremendous
"atmosphere" about really good sea-trout fishing in
the long silent twilight and transparent darkness of the
West Highlands in June and July; something which I
think cannot be experienced anywhere else. If anyone
has never had the chance of this sort of fishing, perhaps
a few remarks might not be too boring.

In the first place, I think a longish rod, say eleven
feet or ten feet six inches, is preferable to a short rod,
and one that has what the tackle-makers call a "wet-fly
action". A long rod is useful because it is often necessary to make rather long casts, and with a short rod
one is apt to have a great deal of line in the water when
a fish is hooked, which is definitely awkward when
dealing with a big sea trout that jumps continuously.

A slightly "whippy" rod is required, because when
sea trout are really taking properly during their
infrequent "evening rises", they more often than not
start the proceedings with a most savage "jag",
followed instantly by a fast rush of about twenty yards,
ending in a jump, so that with a stiff rod one is very
apt to be broken. These are very minor points, but
they are of some help to anyone who has not had much
experience.

Many people advocate the use of only one fly for
this evening fishing, and I think there is much to be
said for the idea, although I must own that I have,
myself, usually used two or even three flies. If the sea
trout are really taking well, undoubtedly one fly is

better and safer, but if they are inclined to be "dour", which is their usual wont, I think two or more flies gives one a better chance of hooking a fish or two.

To illustrate what may happen with droppers on a cast, I must recall a lonely and tragic night I once experienced on the Shiel of Moidart.

The sea trout were very dour that night, and I had not managed to connect with a single fish. I was fishing a lovely open length of the river called Cliff, and had just finished casting from one of the planks which we had erected to enable us to cast well out over the water without wading. Just below me was another plank platform, and it was my habit to leave my line in the water while I walked off one plank and out on to the lower one.

This night, as I walked off the plank with my line dragging in the river behind me, I suddenly felt a most furious tug which nearly pulled me over backwards. What had happened was that for no apparent reason a *salmon* had been following the flies and had taken at the moment I turned round to walk off the plank. Anyway, I found myself into a salmon with a very "whippy" rod, and a rather fine sea-trout cast.

I was fishing with a Peter Ross on the tail, and an Invicta as a dropper. After a few minutes, I realized that my salmon was not only a salmon but about the biggest fish I had ever hooked on the Shiel.

I knew this because he came right into the shallow water near my feet during one part of the proceedings. He was at least thirty pounds, probably nearer thirty-five pounds, and my "whippy" rod had very little influence upon him.

Briefly stated, this adventure went on for over an hour, from about ten-thirty until about a quarter to twelve. Once or twice I believed that my fish was beginning to tire, but each time he soon showed me how wrong I was.

And then after all this bother and anxiety the end came. The salmon made a very long slow run upstream and across into the ever-gathering darkness, and without any apparent reason at all the line was slack and he was gone!

What had happened was that he had taken the Invicta dropper and had been trailing the Peter Ross all over the Shiel river for an hour or more.

When he finally made the long run upstream, he had, as I found out afterwards, gone right through a solid mass of weed near the far bank. The tail fly had, of course, got hung up, and that was that!

If you are fishing a shallow "tail" at night—which is often the very best place—it is almost fatal to use a dropper, as the tail fly invariably gets caught up among the stones when you are running a fish that has taken the dropper. Therefore I am sure that one rather large fly such as a Blue and Silver "low-water" salmon fly is about the best thing one can use in this twilight fishing. A big hackled Butcher can also be very killing.

On some rivers a Connemara Black is much used, but if sea trout are really taking, I do not think the type of fly matters very much as long as it is pretty large.

It is very necessary to carry always a *reliable* torch when night fishing, as, although you may not need it (on the West Coast particularly) you must remember that you probably have some distance to walk home, possibly over tricky ground *after* your fishing is over.

When fishing English or Welsh rivers from July onwards a torch becomes your most treasured possession!

I have twice been miserably lost in really inky darkness, once on the West Coast at about 2 a.m., and once in Wales about midnight. On each occasion my wretched torch failed to work, and I experienced half an hour or more of the most heating and undignified groping before I managed to find in one case a lane, and in another a railway line.

Another factor which assumes on occasions the most heart-rending proportions is *Midges*. This matter of midges used to be a major problem in West-Highland rivers at one time, and on the Shiel we used to wear nets, veils and various other forms of armour, soaked in "Citronella" or some other only slightly effective essence!

Recently, since the latest war instalment, various D.D.T. creams have been produced, which had almost eliminated this menace. . . . Even so, it is necessary to "make-up" pretty heavily with this cream in places where the midges are really bad, and to renew the "make-up" every half an hour or so.

Incidentally, you are likely to have a good night with the sea trout if the midges are really ferocious. The reason for this, I think, a matter of temperature. On hot, still, "muggy" nights sea trout seem to move much more freely than on chilly or windy nights. If there is a touch of frost in the air you might as well go home. When the mist begins to rise, like smoke from the river, the sea trout "go down" at once, and stay there. . . .

Apart from a few little hints of this sort, I do not think there are any known rules about night sea-trout fishing. It is largely a matter of weather, temperature —and luck. Bright moonlight is usually bad for sea-trout fishing. Sometimes (which is quite typical of sea trout fishing in general) it is very good.

Nevertheless, as I have said before, there is no time more exciting and delightful than when, just now and then, in many years perhaps, you find yourself on some quiet dim "tail" of a West-Highland river at about eleven-thirty with the big sea trout slashing savagely at your fly every time you cast.

A friend of mine once had eighteen sea trout on Cliff (on the Shiel) within an hour, all of them were over two pounds, and the largest was over eight pounds. . . . But how seldom—how very seldom—one can hope for this!

CHAPTER XV

SOME SUGGESTIONS AS TO WHERE TO FISH FOR SEA TROUT

IT would require a book of considerable length to mention in detail even a few of the many places where sea trout can be caught in England, Wales, Scotland and Eire. Numberless fishermen have had infinitely more experience of this sort of fishing than I have, so, in this brief chapter, I will mention just a few of the places where I know the fishing *can* be quite good and one or two places where it can be absolutely first class.

I have never, as far as I can remember, caught a sea trout in England, but I believe the Test, below Romsey, can be very good indeed and there are, of course, any amount of places where sea trout are caught occasionally, but personally when I think of sea trout fishing my mind flies immediately to one or two places that I have fished.

In South Wales, between Newcastle Emlyn and Cardigan on the Teifi is a curiously fascinating place of rocks, foaming narrow gullets and a wide quiet little-fished weir. This amazingly beautiful place is called Cenarth, and I shall remember it because of one blazing July day when I watched the most amazing run of small sea trout going up one of the smaller falls, that I have ever seen on any river. There had been a big, sudden flood the day before, caused by a thunderstorm up by Tregaron, and the river was big, and still rather coloured. The sea trout were milling about below the little fall literally in hundreds. I and one or two of the locals tried everything we could think of, but I never hooked a single fish. I found the Teifi generally a very dour river and one, moreover, that has been almost ruined by incessant netting and poaching with salmon-roe.

Once or twice I have had a most exciting night's fishing, in one place and one place only, which any keen and athletic novice may discover for himself if he will stop his car on the bridge at Cenarth and use his "natural genius". . . .

Within 200 yards of that bridge is a place where, if the fisherman does not mind getting wet, risking his life, and getting torn to pieces by brambles, he may enjoy an hour or two's fishing from about ten-thirty at night until twelve o'clock, the like of which he will probably never encounter again in these islands.

Here, to begin with, is a place worth visiting. For the Teifi fishing generally, whether you are after salmon or only sea trout, or both, it is quite essential to consult one Tommy Davies, a true and honest fisher, and a person who really loves to talk about his own most beautiful river. He may be found quite easily in the town of Newcastle Emlyn, where, when he isn't fishing, he attends to the business of his saddler's shop. He can also provide you with everything you need for fishing the Teifi.

If you travel northwards from the Teifi you will arrive in time at another admirable river, the Dovey. Here at Machynlleth is to be found one of the really good sea-trout fisheries of Wales. The Towy of Carmarthen is another very famous Welsh river where the sea trout run very big, but for really first-class sea-trout fishing I think the Dovey is better.

The trout of the Dovey run very big, and I have heard of some really remarkable night fishing. The secretary of the New Dovey Fishery Association would give all information, and I believe day and weekly tickets can be procured if there are not too many rods on the water. It is mostly night fishing, I believe.

I have never fished here, but from the look of the water I should think it an ideal place to try both the thread-line minnow method and the upstream lob-worm technique.

Most of these Middle and North Welsh rivers are very good on occasions for sea trout; the Glasslyn, I know, can be excellent, also the Mawddach near Dolgelley, but I would always make straight for the Gwydyr fishing of the Conway, if I happened to be in those parts.

I think the Conway and the Lledr are about the best all-round rivers both for salmon and sea trout in Wales. The Lledr is not so good as the Conway, as when the sea trout do manage to get up through the endless wild gorges which are a feature of this little river, they are rather past their best.

The Conway, however, is another matter altogether. From the tidal pools below Llanrwst and Trefrw right up to the junction of the Conway and Lledr at the pool of Tyn-y-Cai there is no better sea-trout river in England or Wales.

The very efficient fishing association organized by Mrs. Smith of the Gwydyr Hotel, Bettws-y-Coed, controls the greater part of the fishing on the Conway, and for about 12s. 6d. per day one can fish miles of the very best type of sea-trout water. There is some excellent sea-trout fishing at and below Llanrwst but for this fishing you should consult Mr. Mackintosh at his tackle shop in the town.

Between the highest point reached by the tide below Llanrwst and the Wall Pool, between Bettws-y-Coed and Llanrwst, are some really splendid sea-trout flats. From the Wall Pool upwards on the Association water there are some of the finest sea-trout casts to be found anywhere.

The Conway between Bettws-y-Coed and Llanrwst is, to my mind, quite perfect for day-time minnow fishing, and for night fishing there are several short lengths which are almost perfect.

When one crosses over from Wales to Lancashire, some quite good sea-trout fishing can be had up the Hodder at Whitewell in Bowland. This is a delightful district, but the fishing is not as good as formerly. Much water has been taken from the Hodder for various water schemes and in dry summers the river is apt to become almost hopelessly low.

The Ribble and the Lune are also sea-trout rivers of some note, but personally I would go further north to that very notable sea-trout river, the Border Esk.

Here, between Longtown and the tidal water and the wonderful pools and runs above and below Cannonbie, is to be found some of the best sea-trout fishing in Britain. If you fish from the hotel at Metalbridge, near Longtown, you will quite certainly enjoy very remarkable sport with herling after July, but for the big sea trout I would advise the fisherman to go up to the Cross Keys at Cannonbie, between Longtown and Langholm.

There is no keener or more knowledgeable sea-trout fisher on the Border than Mr. Miller of the Cross Keys Hotel. The salmon fishing here can be quite good in the spring, but it is as a sea-trout fishing that this part of the Esk is really first class.

At the Cross Keys Mr. and Mrs. Miller do really look after their guests. This is one of the few hotels where one can not only be really comfortable, but at the same time enjoy exceptionally good fishing, especially between June and September.

When passing through Carlisle the seeker after the elusive sea trout should not fail to call on Messrs. Strong, who are the main tackle-dealers in this area. They can frequently get a day or two's fishing on some of the very celebrated private sea-trout lengths on the Esk such as "Thompson's Water".

During the second half of June it is sometimes possible to have remarkable fishing, when the shoals of big sea trout are fresh run from the tide. It was on "Thompson's Water" (in those days known as "Monkhouse's Water") that a certain famous Mr Melrose of York (who walked up root-fields for partridges when over 100 years old) caught some record bags of herling and sea trout to his own rod, at the mature age of ninety-five.

And now, when we are over the Border into Scotland, one's choice in sea-trout fishing becomes almost embarrassingly wide. One might go east and try the peculiar estuary fishing at Newburgh, at the mouth of the Ythan in Aberdeenshire. This is peculiar and not very romantic fishing, but at the Udney Arms you can be sure of being comfortable and also be sure to catch any amount of herling, if not many big sea trout. This is one of the most perfect places for practising the thread-line worm technique.

If we prefer the south-western area, there is delightful fishing to be had very cheaply in Galloway.

This lovely corner of Scotland, which is definitely "highland" without being "the Highlands", seems to escape the main tide of the tourist traffic. In some ways the mountains of Galloway are wilder and more remote than most parts of the northern Highlands.

In behind Cairnsmore of Fleet and Merrich, those quiet, brooding and rarely visited mountains, is a wild, almost roadless country of racing burns, dark, sinister gorges and quiet lochs. Out of this lovely wilderness of mountain and whispering heather flow a few really delightful rivers, the Dee of Kirkcudbright, the Nith, the Fleet, the Cree and the Luce of Glen Luce, the Don, the Stinchar and the Girvan, and many smaller rivers. Of these, I think the Dee is probably the least good as far as sea trout are concerned. For salmon these Galloway rivers are mostly "late", i.e., the best runs of fish usually take place in late autumn when the fish are getting red.

For sea trout, the Luce is, I think, one of the really good rivers of Scotland, and, as is not surprising, is not to be fished by the casual visitor. However, I believe it is possible to obtain brief "lets" by application to the local Estate Office.

For a few days quiet and interesting fishing one could do no better than to stop at the little town of Gatehouse, and put up at the Murray Arms, where the proprietor is always ready to advise one about the fishing. If the visitor will call upon Mr. McMurray in the High Street, who, if the river is low will be found examining the mysterious organisms of watches and clocks in his shop, he will learn all that is to be known about the fishing of Galloway.

Mr. McMurray, who runs the local fishing association, is himself a true fisher and a notable sea-trout expert, and is always ready to welcome a fellow fisher.

The Fleet is definitely a "flood river" and fishes best

Robert M. Adam

LOCH SHIEL, VIEW FROM THE SOUTH-WEST (SLOPE OF BEN RESIPOL)

J. D. Rattar

"THE LAST LOCH IN BRITAIN." THE LOCH OF CLIFFE, ISLAND OF UNST, SHETLAND

right at the height of a full spate. I have seen Mr. McMurray hooking big sea trout on a fly when I, in my ignorance, did not think it worth while to try even with a worm.

Curiously enough, I never did much good on the Fleet with a minnow at any height of water, but I think it would be an ideal river for the upstream casting of a lobworm.

There is also a charming little loch up near Gatehouse station, Loch Whyneon, which is well worth fishing for brown trout. I know very little about the sea trout of the Cree, the Stinchar or the Girvan, but I know the Nith can be quite excellent on occasions near Dumfries.

By the way, the Luce is the famous little river referred to by Augustus Grimble in his *Salmon Rivers of Scotland* as the scene of that almost legendary night when a friend of his hooked and landed 100 sea trout. This, I believe, still stands as a record.

And from here onwards, travelling north and west or north and east, the choice of sea-trout fishings becomes too wide to mention in detail.

Many of the places which I have already mentioned for brown trout fishing are also excellent sea-trout centres. The sea-trout fishing in the Hebrides is, of course, very good indeed. The Lochboisdale and Loch Maddy fishings are famous and a visitor to the Tarbert Hotel in Harris can always be sure of any amount of good fishing.

The best way to enjoying good sea-trout fishing is to wander about the North-Western Highlands in a car, making inquiries and having odd days here and there. The boat-fishing in Loch Maree, if you stay at the Loch Maree Hotel, is sometimes quite excellent, if you like sea-trout fishing in a big loch.

I

The Acharacle Hotel at the Moidart end of Loch
Shiel is very comfortable indeed, and Mr. Cameron
will always give all information about the fishing in
the loch.

In Loch Shiel at the Glenfinnan end, where you can
stay at the Stage House, is very good sometimes, both
for salmon and sea trout. This fishing can be easily
reached by train from Fort William.

Apart from the fishing, Glenfinnan is, I think, one
of the most beautiful (and wettest) places in all the
Highlands. To stand by the rather forlorn monument
at the loch head which commemorates the unfurling
of Prince Charles Edward's standard in 1745 is to see
the real heart of the Gaelic Highlands in all their
unforgettable beauty, and sadness.

As a complete contrast to the still and misty twilight
fishing of the West Highlands, there can be nothing more interesting than the sea-trout fishing of
Shetland.

The best months in Shetland are definitely August
and September. The sea trout shoals do not seem to
come into the voes very much before August, and
September is much the best month. In September
also the snipe shooting is beginning to be really
good.

The best way to set about fishing in Shetland is to
take the steamer from Leith or Aberdeen and go first
to the St. Magnus Hotel at Hillswick on the main
island. The good ship "St. Magnus" will take you
direct to Hillswick, where the hotel is all that could be
desired.

It would be wearisome to detail all the voes and
lochs that can be fished from here or Scalloway, but
any visitor will find that a full month's stay will be
far too short for the fishing of half of them. After a

stay on the mainland, I would advise the visitor to take ship from Lerwick on the celebrated "Earl of Zetland", that is the only (almost) link between the North Islands of Shetland and the rest of the world, and journey to Baltasound in Unst.

In this most northerly of the British Isles is to be found every sort of fishing, both for brown trout and sea trout, both in lochs and sea voes. The snipe shooting in Unst is also quite remarkable.

Loch Cliff, a mile or two in from Baltasound, is a very fine brown-trout loch, where one can also hope for a few sea trout to help out a day of, maybe, twenty or thirty nice half-pounders. To wade out and fish the bay of Burrafirth which, by the way, is connected to Loch Cliff by a small burn, is an experience in itself. The shallow, weedy head of the voe at Baltasound is a place where one can have remarkable fun with a thread-line and a cast lobworm, as I have already mentioned. The beach at Uyeasound is also a very good place on occasions. If it can be arranged, the best place to stay at in Unst is with Mrs. Edmondson at her house of Buness in Baltasound. If this is not possible, the Nord Hotel caters for fishermen. Practically all the fishing is free, but the snipe-shooting may cost a small amount.

*   *   *   *   *

It is a far cry from the Test below Romsey to the wild voes of Unst, but wherever there are sea trout to be caught, the true and free fisher will find happiness and beauty, for there is, I contend, nothing in wild Nature more lovely than a fresh-run sea trout as he leaps clear of the water like a flash of burnished silver.

As Andrew Lang, that true fisher, once sang:

". . . Dreamed of the singing showers that break
And sting the lochs or near or far
And rouse the trout and stir the 'take'
 From Urigil to Lochinvar. . . .

Dreamed of the kind propitious sky
O'er Ari Innes brooding grey;
The sea trout rushing at the fly
Breaks the Black Wave with sudden spray!"

CHAPTER XVI

ON COARSE FISH AND THE
STUDY OF QUIETNESS

OF all field sports I believe that fishing is the least class-conscious, and yet even among those who "study to be quiet" there has grown up over the years certain quite perceptible prejudices and divisions and occasionally rather more than a hint of snobbishness.

Even in the term "coarse fishing" one seems to sense a faint tinge of condescension or depreciation. As among dry-fly fishermen the man who catches chub on wasp-grub, or lures the dour barbel with a lobworm is apt to be classed, mentally, as a coarse fellow, to whom the refinements of fly hatches and sailing may-flies are incomprehensible: he who deceives the noble fario with the same wasp-grub or lobworm is merely a vandal.

In the same way, the peaceful and happy exponents of fly fishing are apt to appear as somewhat decadent aristocrats to the silent and knowledgeable experts of the famous roach swims.

The deep wading and deeply experienced casters of downstream wet-flies of the North and West are very apt to belittle those who crawl about in the water meadows of Wessex for the undoing of a brace of nice two-pounders.

The Northern pundits speak slightingly of "tame trout" and "canal fishing" when the limpid waters of Test or Avon are under discussion.

The men of Stockbridge and Kintbury murmur deprecatingly of the "chuck and chance it" methods of our "rough Northern streams". And so it goes on, this quite illogical and rather absurd segregation of the various branches of a peaceful and harmless sport.

Let us for a moment look at the whole subject objectively, if that is possible. To my mind it is quite wrong to speak of "game fish" or "coarse fish' when one considers fishing as a sport. A five-pound chub, hooked on a fly, and a 5X cast is a very game fish indeed; a red and enfeebled autumn salmon hooked on a large fly and a thick cast, and bullied by a sixteen-feet split-cane rod is very far from being game.

A great Mayfly-glutted four-pound trout is frequently a poor thing when hooked, and a bloated horror two hours after he is caught, while a four-pound barbel hooked on the same tackle (with a lob-worm substituted for a large Mayfly) in a fast stream is a worthy opponent indeed, and a thing of beauty when landed.

I have argued on this subject with very many fellow fishers, and have been amazed by the frequency of the remark, when maybe chub or barbel are under discussion, "But you can't *eat* them." . . .

Now this is quite fantastic, this suggestion that we fish in order to eat. It is the resurrection of the primitive to justify the civilized. . . . Just imagine the keen but dyspeptic fisher of some fabled beat of the Dee being forced to feed heavily every day on the salmon he catches; or a member of the Houghton Club returning a five-pounder because he felt sure it would not be good to eat. And yet I have met quite a number of fishers who professed to feel no pleasure in the catching of even enormous chub on a dry-fly because the honest chevern is admittedly quite revolting as an article of food.

The same thing applies to the barbel. Here is one of the most difficult fish to catch—he is frequently of a notable size, and is always and ever one of the finest and gamest fighters among fresh-water fish—which because he cannot be eaten by an ordinary human being is relegated to the under world of "only a coarse fish". . . .

The whole thing is quite unfair, I think, and a matter that all true and free fishers should try to alter.

In actual fact, coarse fishing at its best approaches much more nearly to the true ideal of angling, as demonstrated by the writings and personality of Master Walton himself, than most other types of fishing. The man who sits, perhaps for hours, by some still green pool in high summer, watching his float or rod-tip, sees and hears more of wild Nature and is closer to the great god Pan himself than the heated crawler in water meadows of Wessex, or the athletic wader of the fords of Tweed. He is, in fact, studying to be quiet, which is a very right and proper thing to study in this mid-twentieth century.

For those who value quietness in a noisy and nerve-racked world, let us dwell for a moment on some of the ways in which one can enjoy fishing of a really unfashionable sort.

*   *   *   *   *

I have always loved the graceful and silvery dace since the days, long ago, when I first learnt to cast a fly over the shoals that swam in the deep water of the lower Swale behind my old home in Yorkshire.

The dace is undoubtedly a charming little fish, and

well worth fishing for. At home in Yorkshire and on
the Thames backwaters near my old school, I used
to catch any number of dace, using a short, very light
rod, a 5X cast and a very small black-gnat fly. It has
always seemed to me that good dace fishing with a fly
is quite as much fun as the catching of small trout. In
each case the pleasure of the sport lies more in the
"atmosphere" and surroundings than in the fishing
itself.

It is a very lovely thing to wander up a sun-dappled
little river that sings far down in some Devonshire
combe, but it is also a very pleasant thing to glide
quietly along a Thames backwater in a canoe on a hot
July day, watching the dace shoals, the darting
minnows or an occasional school of basking chub.

I have been told that I have something of a mania
for the honest chub, and I must own there is some
reason for the contention. I have, I suppose, caught
many more big trout than I have chub, but I can
truthfully say that I have had almost as much fun
catching big chub as big trout. I would go further and
say that I would much sooner fish for really big chub
with a dry-fly than for small trout. I have, in fact,
been broken, in fair fight, as it were, very much more
frequently by big chub than by big trout. When one
hooks a three-pound trout with a dry-fly, I find that
one nearly always has a second or two of time in which
to "get organized"; in the case of a hooked chub of
the same weight it is very different. A chub when
hooked almost always makes a most devastating dive
right down to the bottom, which I always find quite
hard to deal with.

In any case, I would advise those who are unable to
reach or afford really good trout-fishing to make a
trial of this most pleasant type of fishing.

Apart from fly-fishing, it is possible to catch chub in various ways. In a fast stream where there are chub, the threadline caster of a minnow will find that he can sometimes have great sport.

On the lower Swale, in Yorkshire, there used to be remarkable shoals of chub each summer, and we had a particular way of fishing for them which was rather amusing.

We used to go down to the river equipped with ordinary float-tackle, and carrying buckets of wasp-grub combs, which we did *not* bake before use.

The drill was as follows: Firstly, large pieces of wasp-grub combs were hurled out on to the water after being bruised and broken by hand. We then retired downstream to a point about 100 yards below where the wasp-grub combs had been thrown in. The big chub, we found, were not slow to discover the nice grub-shedding combs as they floated down, and we nearly always had some really good fun for half an hour or so.

I remember that we once caught four chub—all over three pounds—in a quarter of an hour. The best chub I ever landed on the Swale was just over five pounds, and in this instance I was using a very old 5X cast, and a big "palmer" fly.

*   *   *   *   *

For years now I have been fascinated by the tales I have read and heard about the giant carp of Mapperley and elsewhere, but I have never managed actually to fish for these monsters.

It seems to me that here is a sport which is probably the most difficult and delicate of all angling exercises. I think the idea of hooking and landing a twenty-

or twenty-five-pound fish in heavily weeded water on a 4X or 5X cast is definitely worth studying.

The whole "atmosphere" of this carp-fishing seems to me quite perfect in its setting of quietness, essential knowledge and subtle approach. It would seem to me quite certainly a cult for the Initiates and Masters. Before long I hope to have some slight experience of it.

*   *   *   *   *

I know something of the smaller but equally long-descended tench. As a boy I used to haunt a strange and very ancient pond in a certain lovely park, in which vast and mysterious monsters sometimes moved among the crowded stems of the water-lilies.

A very small boy soon discovered that a tiny worm lowered gently in front of a dark shadow which was in fact a basking tench, on a hot July day, was often the prelude to homeric battles with really magnificent fish.

I lost many more tench than I ever landed, but I shall never forget the thrill of seeing my first big tench, a really big one of nearly five pounds, lying gasping on the bank.

Some of the best places for big tench are the deserted reaches of unused canals, of which there are quite a few in various parts of the country, and there is no pleasanter way of "wasting" a really hot and somnolent afternoon in late June or early July than to stalk and fish for basking tench.

Like the chub, the tench usually goes away with a tremendous dash the moment he is hooked, and as the very finest of tackle is absolutely necessary, the odds are nearly always on the fish and not the fisherman—which is quite as it should be.

*   *   *   *   *

Despite the rude jeers of my friends, I still maintain that the best all-round fish we have in our rivers is *the Eel*. Very many years ago I made the interesting discovery that the eel, when fished for and caught in a sporting manner, is the dourest and most resourceful fighter of all fresh-water fish.

I developed a certain technique for eel fishing which has for many years provided me with much amusement and sport when all other forms of fishing were extremely futile if not absolutely impossible.

I always used, as a boy, a very small weak green-heart fly rod on which an eel of a pound or one and a half pounds put up as good a fight, and took as long to land as many a salmon played on a fourteen-feet rod.

I once had experience of this when I hooked a vast eel on a sixteen-feet Hi Regan salmon rod. . . . I have rarely, if ever, had such an arm-aching thirty-five minutes before I and my ghillie finally managed to land and execute the monster. This particular eel was somewhere about eight pounds in weight, but I am quite convinced that he had the strength of a thirty-pound salmon.

Whenever and however the uninitiated are fishing for eels I would suggest that they have ready a very sharp knife *and* a well thought out drill for dealing with the eel, when it has been landed. The best way is to hold the eel down with the left foot, hold the gut taut with the left hand, and sever (or try to do so) its back bone at the base of its head.

Do not make any attempt to unhook an eel *before* this rather murderous exercise has been carried out, or chaos of a most distressing sort will be your portion.

An eel of a pound or over is, I am convinced, the very best eating fish that can be caught in fresh water, the noble salmon not excepted. My natural greed, where justly and reverently stewed eels are concerned tempts me to record a simple and pleasant recipe which my wife has evolved for my delight.

Skin the eel, being very careful to cut off all the fine spines of the long tail-fins which will remain after skinning. Cut the skinned eel up into convenient small pieces. Lightly brown these pieces in a little fat. Remove the pieces from the pan. Fry slices of onion in the fat. Add one tablespoonful of seasoned flour, mix to a smooth paste. Then add water to make a nice, brown, rather thick gravy.

Replace the pieces of eel in the gravy and add a "bouquet garni" and a small piece of bay leaf.

Simmer gently for about thirty minutes, remembering that *boiling* will bring utter ruin to a very lovely "dish of meat" as Izaak Walton would have remarked.

The addition of a very small amount of good sherry is a delightful refinement, but the flavour of the eel itself when cooked in this simple manner is almost perfect in itself.

*   *   *   *   *

Although my own methods of coarse fishing are anything but gregarious, I must not fail to mention that great and honoured sect of the angling cult, who band themselves into great guilds or clubs, and who move by platoons, regiments and army corps— usually on Saturdays, Sundays and holidays—towards the deep slow rivers or the narrow black canals of their delight. In East Anglia, I believe, these remarkable people even fish in the "drains". . . .

In this powerful sect are very many interesting types. Some are seen to throw great quantities of farinaceous

matter into the water to be fished. Others cast upon
the waters endless millions of maggots; others, again,
have an almost mystic belief in cheese.

There are, moreover, certain peculiarities common
to all these guild-fishers. All of them maintain an air
of almost criminal cunning whenever fishing is mentioned; they also, without exception, carry with them
when fishing enormous quantities of tackle, personal
belongings and nourishment.

These tens of thousands of honest men and fishermen,
sufferers, one might almost say, from the great Canal
Delusion, who, through long and silent week-ends
watch floats (what do they care if those floats rarely
move; if the roach and bream, sated with vast doles of
dough and maggots, enjoy full-fed siestas down among
the weeds) what indeed do they care? For these
peaceful and philosophical "wage-slaves" have for a
brief few hours forgotten all about foremen and shop-
stewards, the great-lunged leaders of their union
meetings, and the warm-hearted and courteous philan-
thropists of the Labour Exchange.

For hours and hours, these poor and downtrodden
earners of a mere ten pounds or so a week forget all
about "anomalies", "victimization" and "bonus
rates". Only the brainless and scuttering moorhens
disturb their peaceful reveries, and the far-off notes
of the village clock, which tells them that "they are
open". . . .

They live in a world which might to some seem
crazy and pointless, these static men, for long hours
each summer week-end, but on Monday at 7.30 they
will be sane again—or will they?

They are, in very fact, quite amazing people, these
contenders for sweepstakes and prizes, for salad bowls
and "fish knives and forks" and watches, but they are

also by far the largest body of anglers in this country and, moreover, true lovers of fishing.

Personally, I should hate to fish in the company of some hundreds of other anglers, however honest, but I would sooner fish in an "All England" Competition than not fish at all.

When Coarse Fishing is spoken about with contempt or preciousness by the purists of the chalk streams, or the slayers of spring salmon, let it be remembered that the vast majority of Britons who fish, fish with floats or legers; with writhing maggot or sinuous lobworm and that they too are Free Fishers and true Waltonians.

THE FISHING VISITOR IN BRITAIN

ONE of the most outstanding peculiarities of fishermen is their astonishing ignorance of the fishing to be enjoyed in other countries. One, but only one, of the reasons for this is probably the language difficulty—few fishing books or guides reach the eminence of being translated. And yet, even those nations who speak the same language seem to know very little of each other's sport. A notable attempt to remedy this was made by Mr. Negley Farson, in his excellent book *Going Fishing*, which must have been read with pleasure by fishermen all over the English-speaking world.

As an Englishman, I am well aware that the English, as a race, are quite remarkable in their lack of knowledge of fishing and fish culture in any country but their own. In fact, this peculiarity is not confined to fishing. I can personally vouch for the utter astonishment for a very well-known fox-hunting man, when he was informed that there were more packs of hounds in the United States than in England.

The backwardness of Britain in fish culture and fish farming is also quite amazing. Members of our Control Commission in Germany were astounded—almost shocked, one might say—when confronted by the very admirable and successful hunting laws attributable largely to Hermann Goering.

Despite the fact that they are all within a few hours

flying-time of London, very few British fishermen have
the faintest knowledge of the excellent rivers and lakes
of France, Belgium or Austria. In Brittany and
Finisterre, in the neighbourhood of such places as
Quimper, there is excellent salmon and sea-trout
fishing, resembling almost exactly the fishing of the
West of Scotland, and the Hebrides, but few Britons
would ever think of sea trout in connection with
Western France. Even the Shetland Isles are only
slightly known to most British fishermen, although a
fishing and snipe-shooting visit to Shetland is an
almost unique experience. The almost incredibly pure
air of these northern islands is literally "like wine",
and has much the same effect when one first goes there.
There is something about those pale green islands in
the deepest of deep blue seas, and the flash of wheeling
squadrons of golden plover against the great slope of
Saxaford in Unst, that is unforgettable; and yet comparatively few Britons visit Shetland.

Canadians and Australasians, on the other hand,
are apt to have an idea that the fishing in Canada or
New Zealand is infinitely superior to British fishing.
Few foreigners, except, of course, those Americans who
spend much time and very many extremely welcome
dollars in Scotland or Ireland, realize the amazingly
good fishing to be had on the Tweed, the Aberdeenshire Dee, or the Spey. On the Tweed, for example,
each spring it is quite usual for ten or twelve salmon,
averaging say ten pounds, to be caught in one day's
fishing by a single rod. Catches of twenty or more fish
are not unknown.

In Lewis, in the Hebrides, is another remarkable
fishing—the Grimersta river and lochs. Here the
catches of salmon, averaging about six or seven
pounds, are extraordinary. I believe that the record

Robert M. Adam

RIVER EWE, NEAR POOLEWE, NORTH-WEST ROSS

A. K. Brennand

THE PLACE OF BASKING CHUB

for the Grimersta is something over fifty salmon in one day. Of course, like almost everywhere in the world, these exceptional fishings are very much sought after, and correspondingly expensive.

British fishing seems to swing from the sublime to the ridiculous. Thousands of keen fishermen take infinite pains, and expend a great deal of money, to fish rivers and lochs where the average size of the trout is absurdly small—probably under half a pound, or to fish for salmon in places where a whole season's catch will not equal one good day on Tweed or Dee. Others, as I have said before, think nothing of catching forty or fifty salmon in a few days' fishing.

On the very specialized and closely preserved chalk stream fishings of Hampshire, Wiltshire and Berkshire, the average of brown trout caught is very high—over two pounds in some places. On these small, clear rivers four-pound or five-pound trout are quite usual. In this sort of fishing, where the trout are fished for with a small floating fly, gossamer thin gut-casts, and tiny four-ounce rods, a very considerable degree of skill and experience is required. On the other hand, on most of the northern and border rivers, there is apt to be more quantity than quality in a day's bag.

I think that many visiting anglers from overseas are very prone to confuse these widely different sorts of trout fishing.

In Australia, Ceylon, Kenya Colony and on many Canadian fishings, much of the fishing is of the fast, rough stream type—much resembling, superficially, the fishings of our northern rivers, where one or more sunken flies are used on a cast, and the fishing is mostly done down-stream. In New Zealand, Australia, or Canada, and many other places, trout up to six pounds are often caught. It will be understood, there-

K

fore, that an overseas fisherman fishing for trout,
say, the Tweed, is somewhat disappointed when he
hooks nothing but fish of half a pound or under. He is
very apt to overlook the fact that in Britain large trout
which are mostly to be found in our southern chalk
streams, are to be caught if the correct methods of
approach and fly presentation are used.

The famous Houghton Club of Stockbridge, which
owns or rents miles of the Test in Hampshire, has an
amazing record over many years, and is a model of
what an English trout fishery should be. It is, of course,
extremely difficult for a casual, visiting angler to get a
day or two on this lovely water.

During the first fortnight of June the trout are
feeding furiously on great hatches of Mayfly or Green
Drakes, so that these few weeks of late May or early
June have come to be looked upon as a kind of carnival
time of trout fishing. On some streams, such as the
Kennet near Hungerford, in Berkshire, very large
trout, up to seven pounds in weight, can be seen rising
during this Mayfly carnival; trout which at any other
season of the year do not appear to rise to surface feed
at all.

The technique of what is called "dryfly fishing" is
generally looked upon as the highest form of fishing to
be enjoyed in Britain. On some of the loughs of Eire,
very large trout are caught each year by means of
what is called "blow-line fishing" or "dapping'. This
is a very amusing and sometimes exciting form of
fishing, which is also at its best when the Mayflies or
Green Drakes are "up". In this form of fishing a very
long rod is used from a boat, and two live Mayflies are
impaled on a tiny single hook, and allowed to "blow"
out over the water before being dropped, or "dapped",
over a rising fish.

The catches of big trout on Loughs Mask or Corrib, and on the West Meath loughs during the "dapping" season, are quite remarkable. In recent years the Tourist Board in Eire have issued several admirable guides and pamphlets on Irish fishing, and they are very much more progressive in this respect than any organization in England or Scotland.

However, I think that the fishing hotels of Scotland, for comfort and service, are very much the best in Britain, even if the actual fishing is not by any means as good as it could be. Within the last few years many sporting estates in Scotland (and in Eire) have been taken over by private hotel companies, and in some of them visitors can enjoy fishing and shooting of a quality quite unobtainable a few years ago by outsiders.

It seems to me that a few articles by experienced fishermen published in such English papers as *The Field* or *Country Life* on the fishing, means of transport, and accommodation in the United States and Canada would be of enormous interest to thousands of fishermen in Britain. The same thing applies to many places in Europe. Recently I have seen a very excellent guide to the fishing of France, but as it is rather naturally written in French, it will not appeal to the majority of British anglers. As is well known, the "honest men and fishermen", as good Master Walton called them, of England and Scotland, are very apt to speak and read only their own peculiar language. It would appear to me an obvious suggestion that this most interesting guide should be translated.

There is one thing, however, which is common to all fishermen, and which transcends all questions of language and customs: they are for the most part happy men ,and the beauty and "atmosphere" of the countries in which they fish and the good talk and companionship in their inn, hotel or camp after the day's fishing is over, means infinitely more to them than the number or size of fish caught.

One of the decorations by C. Walter Hodges from *Halcyon*

Also by GEORGE BRENNAND

HALCYON

AN ANGLER'S MEMORIES

An unusually distinguished book of fishing reminiscences which will be read by anglers and non-anglers for the excellence of its prose style and its refreshing *joie de vivre*.

"This is a delightful book. Mr. Brennand has the enviable gift of being able to convey by his pen . . . that indefinable sense of wellbeing which nearly all of us feel in the presence of running water, but which so few can write down on paper. His fishing has never been on the grand scale . . . an ordinary angler enjoying ordinary sport, but the charm of it is undeniable."

SALMON AND TROUT MAGAZINE

With a frontispiece and decorations by
C. Walter Hodges. 16s. *net*

A Selection of Books on Fishing
published by
ADAM AND CHARLES BLACK

A DICTIONARY OF TROUT FLIES
AND OF FLIES FOR SEA-TROUT AND GRAYLING
by A. Courtney Williams

This new and very comprehensive study supersedes the author's *Trout Flies: A Discussion and a Dictionary*, and has been planned around a much more substantial list of natural and artificial flies. Over 400 carefully selected dressings have been included. "A most valuable book . . . that will be accepted as the standard work on the subject." THE FISHING GAZETTE. Second edition. With 16 plates (8 in colour). 25*s. net*

SUNSHINE AND THE DRY FLY
by J. W. Dunne

"The angler who is disposed to take trouble and tie his own flies will find in this book an astonishing amount of very valuable information." SCOTTISH COUNTRY LIFE. Second edition. With several drawings. 8*s.* 6*d. net*

HOW TO DRESS SALMON FLIES
by T. E. Pryce-Tannatt

The author writes for the beginner, describing in detail the tying of individual patterns from start to finish. The colour plates show salmon flies grouped naturally according to seasonal and local requirements. With 12 plates (8 in colour) and 101 drawings. 15*s. net*

MODERN TROUT FISHING
by W. Carter Platts

"Heartily recommended as giving a really unprejudiced view of the sport in all its phases, and especially to the novice in angling, who will find in it all he needs to know about how, when and where to fish." THE FIELD. Second edition. With 16 plates and 15 drawings.   15s. net

Three books by G. E. M. Skues

MINOR TACTICS OF THE CHALK STREAM

". . . he most undoubtedly raises wet-fly fishing to its highest possible level." DAILY TELEGRAPH. Third edition. With a colour frontispiece.   15s. net

THE WAY OF A TROUT WITH A FLY
AND SOME FURTHER STUDIES IN MINOR TACTICS

". . . of absorbing interest to anyone who studies trout and their surface feeding habits and who casts a fly." SHOOTING TIMES. Fourth edition, revised and enlarged. With 3 plates (2 in colour).   15s. net

NYMPH FISHING
FOR CHALK STREAM TROUT

". . . deals with everything that the nymph fisher may want to know. Let the purists attack him: they will not shake his fame in the eyes of future (and many present) trout fishermen." COUNTRY LIFE. With 16 artificial nymphs in colour, and 2 photographs.   12s. 6d. net

FISHERMAN'S KNOTS AND WRINKLES
by W. A. Hunter

The angler will find here all he needs to know about knots, net-making, fly-tying, fish-modelling, etc. Third edition. With many drawings.   5s. net

THE PRACTICAL ANGLER
OR, THE ART OF TROUT FISHING MORE PARTICULARLY APPLIED TO CLEAR WATER
by W. C. Stewart

This book was originally published in 1857, when it had a great vogue. A revised edition with an introduction by the late Earl Hodgson was issued in 1906, since when the demand has been such that it has been constantly reprinted. With 6 plates of flies in colour.   7s. 6d. net

Two books by H. D. Turing
TROUT PROBLEMS

"A sound, practical and important contribution to angling literature." SHOOTING TIMES. With 16 plates.   15s. net

TROUT FISHING

"His book is extremely comprehensive, and, throughout, the novice is given not only advice but the reasoning by which the opinions expressed are arrived at." JOURNAL OF THE FLY-FISHERS' CLUB. Third edition. With 8 photographs and several drawings.   7s. 6d. net